A Short Account of the Destruction of the Indies

Bartolomé de las Casas

For information regarding special discounts for bulk purchases, please contact BN Publishing at info@bnpublishing.com

CONTENTS

POPERY

Truly displayed in its bloody colors.

A faithful narrative of the horrid and unexampled massacres, butcheries and all manner of cruelties that hell and malice could invent, committed by the Popish Spanish Party on the inhabitants of West-India TOGETHER with the devastations of several Kingdoms in America by fire and sword, for two years, from the time of its first discovery by them.

Composed first in Spanish by Bartholomew de las Casas, a Bishop there, and Eye-Witness of most of these Barbarous cruelties; afterward Translated by him into Latin, then by other hands, into High-Dutch, Low-Dutch, French, and now Taught to Speak Modern English.

PREFACE TO THE READER

The Reverend Author of this compact summary was Bartholomaeus de las Casas – alias: Casaus, a pious and religious person (as appears by his zealous transports in this narrative for promotion of the Christian faith). Elevated from a Friar of the Dominican Order to sit in the Episcopal Chair, he was frequently importuned by good and learned men, particularly Historians, to publish this summary, who so prevailed him, that he collected out of that copious History which might and ought to be written on this subject. The contents of this concise Treatise, with intention to display to the world the enormities the Spaniards committed in America during their residence there, to their eternal ignominy. The author, finding that no admonitions or reprehensions, how mild soever, could operate upon or sink into the rocky-hearted tyrants in those western parts; he therefore took up a firm resolution, being then about 50 years of age (as he himself declares), to run the hazards and dangers by sea at the risk of a long voyage into Spain, to acquaint and certify the illustrious Prince Phillip, the Son and Heir of his Imperial Majesty Charles the Fifth of Blessed Memory, with the horrid crimes perpetrated in those countries, part seen by him and part heard from those who boasted of their wickedness.

When his Majesty moved with a tender and Christian compassion towards the inhabitants of these countries, languishing for want of damages, he called a Council at Valedolid, Anno Dom. in 1542, consisting of learned and able men, in order to reform the West-Indian government, and took such action that from then on, their tyranny and cruelty against the barbarians was somewhat repressed, and those nations - in some measure - delivered from that intolerable and more than Egyptian bondage, or at least the Spaniards ill usage, and treatment of the Americans was alleviated and abated.

This book - mostly historical, part typographical - was published first by the Author in Spanish in Sevil, and after that it was translated into Latin by himself; after time into High Dutch, Low Dutch, French and now English; which is the sixth language. If any nation in this Narrative might contemplate and see as in a mirror the dismal and deadly fruits, thereby learning to abhor and detest it, *Cane pejus & angue*: it being the predominant motive to the commission of such inexpressible outrages, as here in part are faintly but not fully represented. The sin the Pagan Indians expropriate in the Spaniards with loathing, ignominy and disgrace, was when they had taken some of them prisoners (which was rarely), they bound them hand and foot, laid them on the ground and poured melted gold down their throats, as they cried out and called aloud in derision, "Yield, throw up thy gold O' Christian! Vomit and spew out the metal which has so inseminated and envenomed both body and soul, that has stained and infected thy mind with desires and contrivances, and thy hands with commission of such matchless enormities." This is but an Extract of what is in the prefatory part of the original. I earnestly hope and beg you to believe that this summary was not published with private design and sinister ends or affection in favor or prejudice of any particular Nation; but for the public emolument and advantage of moral men throughout the whole world.

Farewell

The cruelties of the Spaniards committed in America

America was discovered and found in 1492, resulting with it being inhabited by the Spaniards, with a multitude of them traveling there from Spain during the next 49 years.

Their first attempt was on the Spanish Island, which has a most fertile soil and, at present, has a great reputation for its spaciousness and length, containing in perimeter 600 miles. It's surrounded by an innumerable number of Islands, which we found well inhabited with natives and foreigners, that there isn't a region in the universe with so many people: but the main land, which is 250 miles north of the Island, extends it self to over 10,000 miles in length near the sea-shore. Some islands are already discovered and more will be found in the process of time.

The amount of people inhabiting these countries, make it seem as if the Omnipotent God has assembled and concocted the major part of mankind in this part of the world.

These multitude of people were created innocently simple, void of and averse to all manner of craft, and are most obedient and loyal Subjects to their Native Sovereigns; behaving very patiently, submissively and quietly towards the Spaniards, to whom they are subservient and subject; living without the least thirst of revenge, laying aside all litigiousness, commotion and hatred.

This is a most tender and effeminate people, and so imbecile and unequal-balanced tempered that they are altogether incapable of hard labor. So much so that in a few years, in one way or other, the very issue of Lords and Princes, who among us live with great affluence, will not be more effeminate and tender than the children of their laborers. This Nation is very necessitous and indigent, Masters of few possessions, and consequently, are neither haughty nor ambitious. They are parsimonious in their diet, as the Holy Fathers were in their frugal life in the desert, known by the name of *Eremites*. They go naked, having no other covering but what conceals their genitalia from public sight. A loose Coat, about 45 inches, or a coarse woven cloth 90 inches long at most, serves them for the warmest winter garment. They lye on a coarse rug or mat, and those that have the most plentiful estate or fortunes, the better sort, use net-work, knotted at the four corners in lieu of eds, which the Inhabitants of the Island of Hispaniola, in their own proper Idiom term: Hammocks. The people are pregnant and docile. The natives are responsive, and capable of morality and goodness, very apt to receive the instilled principles of the Catholic religion; nor are they averse to civility and good manners, being not so much discomposed by the variety of obstructions, as the rest of Mankind; that having sucked in (if I may so express my self) the the very first rudiments of the Christian faith, that they are so transported with zeal and furor in the exercise of ecclesiastical sacraments and divine service, that the very religious themselves, need to undergo the greatest and most impressive patience for such extream transformations. To conclude, I my self have heard the Spaniards themselves (who dare not assume the confidence to deny the good nature predominant in them) declare, that they didn't want any learn about eternal beatitude, only about deity.

The Spaniards first assaulted the innocent sheep, as is premonition, like most cruel and hungry tigers, wolves and lions; studying nothing for forty years, after their first landing, but the massacre of these wretches, whom they have so inhumanely and barbarously butchered and harassed with several kinds of torments, never before known or heard (of which you shall have some account in the following discourse) that of three millions of people, which lived in Hispaniola itself, there is at present only a remnant of scarcely three hundred. So the Isle of Cuba, which extends as far as Valledolid in Spain is distant from Rome, is now uncultivated, like a desert, and entombed in its own ruins. You may also find the Isles of St. John and Jamaica, both large and fruitful places, uninhabited and desolate. The Lucayan

Islands on the North Side, adjacent to Hispaniola and Cuba, (which are number about sixty together with, the vulgarly known by the name of, the Gigantic Isles and others), exceeds the Royal Garden of Sevil in quality, with a healthful and pleasant climate, which is now wild and uninhabited; whereas, when the Spaniards first arrived here, about five hundred thousand people dwelt in it. They were gone now - some by slaughter, and others taken away by force and violence, to work in the Mines of Hispaniola, which had no Native Inhabitants. A ship sailing to this Isle, with the harvest being over (a piety good Christian, undertook this dangerous voyage, to convert others to Christianity) so that the remaining people might be gathered up, that there were only eleven of them left, which I saw with my own eyes. There are other Islands, thirty in number, on the northern border of the Isle of St. John, which are over 2000 miles in length, and yet remain uninhabited.

We are sure that the Spaniards, by their barbarous and wretched actions, have absolutely depopulated as much as ten countries on the main land, all of greater extent than Spain, Arragon and Portugal put together, above 1000 Miles in all. The main land now lays desolate and ruined, when as formerly no other Country whatsoever was more populated.

We dare to affirm, that during the 40 years of the Spanish slaughterous Dictatorship in these Regions, over twelve million (computing men, women, and children) have undeservedly perished; I don't conceive that I deviate from the truth by saying that over fifty million in all paid their last debt to nature.

Those that arrived at these Islands from the remotest parts of Spain, and who pride themselves in the name of Christians, arrived for two primary reasons, to excommunicate and exterminate inhabitants of the Islands from the face of the earth. The first was by raising an unjust, gory and cruel War. The other, by putting to death those who fought for their pristine

13

freedom and shake off the shackles of such an injurious captivity. Only the women and children were permitted to enjoy the benefit of that country-air, while the men went off to war, though they were happy to do so, for the innumerable reasons of their tyranny, in this form, was to extirpate and make this a desolate People. This may be reduced and referred.

Now the ultimate reason for the incited Spaniards endeavor of extirpation and desolation of this People, was gold. Their want of grandeur was such, that they might arrive at once at such degrees and dignities, was in no way consistent with their personalities. This was their need to grow opulent in a short manner of time

Finally, in one word, their ambition and avarice (since the heart of man never entertained greater the vast wealth of those regions) and the humility and patience of the Inhabitants (which made their approach to these Lands more effortless and easy), and much promotion of the business; drove them to behave in such ways, so despicable and condemned, that they treated them (I speak of things which I was an Eye Witness of, without the least fallacy) not as beasts, which I cordially wished they would, but as the most abject dung and filth of the earth. They were so solicitous of their life and soul, that the above-mentioned number of people died without understanding the true faith or Sacraments. This is true to the precedent Narration (which the very Tyrants and cruel Murderers cannot deny without the stigma of a lie), that the Spaniards were received by the Indians, as Persons descended from Heaven, until that they were compelled to take up arms, provoked by repeated injuries, violent torments and injustice butcheries.

Of the Island Hispaniola

On this Isle, as we've said, where the Spaniards first attempt of the bloody slaughter and destruction first began: violently forcing away women and children to make them slaves, ill-treating them by consuming and wasting their food, which they had purchased with great sweat and toil (even that wasn't enough, and very inconsiderably only provided the food absolutely necessary to support nature without superfluity), when one individual Spaniard consumed more food in one day, than would serve to maintain three native families in a month, every one consisting of ten people. Being oppressed by such evil and afflicted with such great torments and violence, they began to understand that the Spaniards are not on a mission from Heaven and therefore concealed their provisions sending them to their wives and children lurking in holes, but some, to avoid the obdurate and dreadful temper of Spaniards, sought their refuge on the rugged Mountain tops. The Spaniards cruelty didn't end with cuffs, blows and wicked cudgeling, but laid violent hands also on the Cities Governors which at the height of the audacious acts a certain captain abused the Consort of the Isles most powerful King. This is how rebellion started to making its way in the minds of the Natives and they immediately took up arms. And, good God, what arms do you think they used? Of course both offensive and defensive resembled reeds, where you fight with one another, more than with manly arms and weapons.

The Spaniards perceived this at once, but they as apposed to the natives, mounted horses, were well weaponed with lances and swords, and began to exercise their bloody Butcheries and Strategies, overrunning their cities and towns, sparing no age or sex, ripping up their bellies, tore them alive in pieces. They laid wagers among themselves, who should with a sword at one blow cut, or divide a man in two; or which of them should decapitate or behead a man, with the greatest dexterity; even farther, which

15

should sheath his sword in the bowels of a man with the quickest dispatch and expedition.

They snatched young babes from the mothers breasts, and then bashed the brains out of those innocents against the rocks; others they cast into rivers scoffing and jeering them, and called upon their bodies when falling with disrespect. This was the true testimony of their cruelty, inhumanely exposing others to their merciless swords, together with the mothers that gave them Life.

They erected certain gibbets, large, but low made, so that their feet almost reached the ground, every one of which was so ordered as to bear thirteen people in honor and reverence (as they said blasphemously) of our Redeemer and his Twelve Apostles, under which they made a fire to burn them to ashes while they hang. But those they intended to preserve alive, they were dismissed, their hands half cut and still hanging by the skin, to carry their letters to those that fly from us and lay skulking on the mountains.

The lords and persons of noble extract were usually exposed to this kind of death; they ordered grid irons to be placed and supported with wooden forks, and putting a small fire under them, these miserable wretches by degrees and with loud shrieks and exquisite torments, at last expired.

I once saw four or five of their most powerful Lords laid on these grid irons, roasted, and not far off, two or three more over-spread with the same commodity, man's flesh; but the shrill clamors which were heard there being offensive to the Captain, by hindering his repose, he commanded them to be strangled with a halter.

The Executioner (whose Name and Parents at Sevil are not unknown to me) prohibited the doing of it; but stopped gags into their mouths to prevent the hearing of the noise (he himself making the fire) till that they died, when they had been roasted as long as he thought convenient.

I was an Eye-Witness of these and and innumerable number of other cruelties: And because all men, who could lay hold of the opportunity, sought out lurking holes in the mountains, to avoid as dangerous rocks so brutish and barbarous a People, strangers to all goodness, and the extirpates and adversaries of men, they bred up such fierce hunting dogs as would devour an Indian like a hog, at first sight in less than a moment. Such kind of slaughters and cruelties as these were committed by the mutts, and if at any time it happened, (which was rarely) that the Indians irritated upon a just account and destroyed or took away the life of any Spaniard, they promulgated and proclaimed this law among them, that one hundred Indians should die for every individual Spaniard that should be slain.

Of the Kingdoms contained in Hispaniola

This Isle of Hispaniola was made up of Six of their greatest Kingdoms, and as many most powerful Kings, to whose Empire almost all the other infinite Lords, did pay their Allegiance.

One of these Kingdoms was called Magua, signifying a campaign or open country; which is very observable, if any place in the Universe deserves taking notice of, and memorable for the pleasantness of its situation; for it is extended 80 miles from South to North, and five to eight (and in some parts ten) miles in length; and is on all sides enclosed with the highest Mountains; above thirty thousand rivers and small streams of water on her Coasts, twelve of which bend in all the magnitude to those famous Rivers, the Eber, Duer, and Guadalquivir; and all those Rivers which have their source or spring from the Mountains lying West, (they number Twenty Thousand) are very rich in Mines of gold; on which Mountain lies the Province of rich Mines, where the exquisite gold of the Twenty Four Carats weight, takes denomination. The King and Lord of this Kingdom

17

was named Guarionex, who governed within the compass of his Dominions so many vassals and potent Lords, that every one of them was able to bring into the field sixteen thousand soldiers for the service of Guarionex their Supreme Lord and Sovereign, when summoned. Some of which I was acquainted with. This was a most Obedient Prince, endued with great courage and morality, naturally peaceful tempered, and most devoted to the service of the Castile's Kings. This King commanded and ordered his Subjects, that every one of those Lords under his Jurisdiction, should present him with a bell full of gold; but in succeeding times, being unable to perform it, they were commanded to cut it in two, and fill one part for the Inhabitants of this Isle, who were altogether inexperienced, unskilful Mine-workers who couldn't dig gold out of the mines. This Guarionex proffered his Service to the King of Castile, on this condition, that he would take care that the lands should be cultivated and manured, where during the reign of Isabella, Queen of Castile, the Spaniards first set foot and fixed their residence, extending it to 50 miles in length even to Santo Domingo. He declared (nor was it a Misconception, but an absolute truth,) that his Subjects were not the practical gold mine diggers. To which promises he had readily and voluntarily condescended, to my own certain knowledge, by this means, the King would have received the annual revenue of three million Spanish Crowns and more, there being at that very time fifty cities more ample and spacious than Sevil it self.

In what way did this Clement and Benign Monarch, can you imagine, reward the Lord do you think? They insulted him in an unimaginable way, when a Spanish Captain altogether unworthy of the Name of Christian, violated his Spouse. He might indeed have expected to meet with a convenient time and opportunity of revenging this Disgrace so injuriously thrown upon him by preparing military forces to attack him, but he rather chose to bolt to the Province De Los Ciquayos (wherein a powerful follower

18

and subject of his Ruled) devastated of his Estate and Kingdom, there to live and die an exile. Upon receiving certain information, the Spaniards found his hiding palce and raised war against him, who had received them with so great humanity and kindness, and having first destroyed the whole Region, at last found and took him prisoner, bound him and shipped him off to Castile as a captive: but the ship perished in the voyage, where many of the Spaniards were lost as well, along with a great weight of gold, among which there was a prodigious Ingot of gold, resembling a large loaf of bread, weighing 3600 Crowns; This is how God revenged their enormous impieties.

A Second Kingdom was named Marien, where there is to this day a haven, upon the utmost borders of the plain or open Country toward the North, more fertile and large than the kingdom of Portugal; and really deserving constant and frequent inhabitants: For it abounds with Mountains, and is rich in Mines of gold and Orichalcum, a kind of Copper Metal mixed with gold; The Kings name of this place was Guacanagari (now Haiti), who had many powerful Lords (some who were not unknown to me) under his subjection. The first that landed in this Kingdom when he discovered America was an Admiral well stricken in years, who had so hospitable and kind a reception from the said Guacanagari, as well as all those Spaniards that accompanied him in that voyage, giving them all imaginable help and assistance (for the admiral's vessel was sunk on their Coasts) that I heard it from his own mouth, he could not possibly have been entertained with greater caresses and civilities from his own parents in his own native country.

But this King being forced to fly to avoid the Spanish slaughter and Cruelty, deprived of all he was Master of, died in the Mountains; and all the rest of the Potentates and Nobles, his subjects, perished in that servitude and Vassalage; as you shall find in this following Treatise.

The Third Kingdom was distinguished by the Denomination of Maquana, another admirable, healthful and fruitful Region, where at present the most refined sugar of the Island is made. Caonabo then reigned there, who surmounted all the rest in Power, State, and the splendid Ceremonies of His Government. This King beyond all expectation was surprised in his own Palace, by the great subtlety and industry of the Spaniards, and after being carried on board in order to be transported to Castile, there being at that time six ships riding in the Haven and ready to set sail, such an impetuous storm suddenly arose, that they - as well as the Passengers and Ships Crew - were all lost, together with King Caonabo loaded with Irons; by which judgment the Almighty declared that this was as unjust and impious an Act as any of the former. This King had three or four Brothers then Living, men of strength and Valor, who being highly incensed at the Captivity of their King and Brother, to which he was injuriously reduced, having also intelligence of the Devastations and Butcheries committed by the Spaniards in other Regions, and not long after hearing of their Brothers death, took up Arms to revenge themselves of the Enemy, whom the Spaniards met with, and certain party of Horse (which proved very offensive to the Indians) made such havoc and slaughter among them, that half of this Kingdom was laid waste and depopulated.

Xaraqua is the fourth Kingdom, and as it were the center and middle of the whole Island, it is not to be equaled for fluency of Speech and politeness of idiom or dialect by any inhabitants of the other Kingdoms, and in Policy and Morality transcends them all. Herein the Lords and Peers abounded, and the very Populace excelled in stature and habit of Body. Their King was Behechio by name and he had a sister called Anacaona, and both loaded the Spaniards with benefits and singular acts of civility, and by delivering them from the evident and apparent danger of Death, did signal services to the Castile's Kings. With Behechio dying, the supreme power of the Kingdom fell to Anacaona: But it happened one day, that the Governor of an Island, attended by 60 Horsemen and 30 Footmen (now the Cavalry was sufficiently able to overtake not only the Isle, but also the whole Continent) summoned about 300 Dynasty's, or Noblemen, to appear before him and commanded the most powerful of them, being first crowded into a thatched Barn or Hovel, to be set on fire, and the rest to be pierced with lances and run through with the point of the Sword, by a multitude of men: And Anacaona her self who (as we said before,) swayed the Imperial Scepter, to her greater honor was hanged on a Gibbet. And if any person, be it by compassion or covetousness, entertained any Indian boys and mount them on Horses to prevent their Murder, another was appointed to follow them to run them through the back or in the hinder parts. If they chanced to escape Death and fall to the ground, they immediately cut off his Legs; and when any of those Indians, that survived these barbarous massacres, fled to an Isle eight miles distant to escape their Butcheries, they were then committed to servitude during Life.

The Fifth Kingdom was Hiquey, over whom Queen Hiquanama, a superannuated Princess, whom the Spaniards crucified, presided and Governed. The number of those I saw here burnt, dismembered and racked with various torments, as well as others, and the poor remnants of such matchless Villainies, who surviving were enslaved, is infinite.

But because so much might be said concerning the assassinations and depopulating of these people, as cannot without great difficulty be published in writing (nor do I conceive that one percent of 1000 that is written here can be fully displayed) I will only add one remark more of the foreboding Wars, in lieu of an aftermath or conclusion, and allege upon my conscience, that notwithstanding all the above named - injustice, profligate enormities and other crimes which I omit (those sufficiently known to me) - the Indians did not, nor was it in their power to authorize them, like the pious religious living in a well regulated monastic life can afford the sacrilegious villains, to deprive them of their Goods and Life or why those who by flight avoided death, should be detained in perpetual, not to be ransomed, captivity and slavery. I add farther, that I really believe and am satisfied by certain undeniable conjectures, that at the very time, when all these outrages were committed on this Isle, the Indians were not guilty of any single mortal sin against the Spaniards that might deserve from any man revenge or require satisfaction. And as for those sins, the punishment that God has reserved for himself as the immoderate desire of revenge, hatred, envy (or inward resentment of spirit) to which they might be transported against such capital enemies as the Spaniards were, I judge that very few of them can justly be accused of them; for their impetuosity and vigor was inferior to that of children of ten or twelve years of age. I can assure you, that the Indians had a just cause of raising war against the Spaniards, and the Spaniards war, on the contrary, was raised injuriously and groundlessly then any undertaken by the worst of Tyrants.

All which I affirm of all their other Transactions and passages in America

With the warlike engagements being over and the Inhabitants all swept away, they divided among themselves the young men, women and Children reserved promiscuously for that purpose. One obtained thirty, another forty, to this Man one hundred were disposed, to the other two hundred, and the more one was domineering with the Tyrant (which they called Governor) the more he became Master of, upon the pretense and provision that he should instruct in the Catholic Religion, when those who were instructed to teach, they themselves were - for the major part - idiots, cruel, covetous, infected and stained with all sorts of vices. This is how they cared for them: the men were sent to the Mines to dig up gold, which is an intolerable labor; and the women were made to work the ground, which is a toil most irksome even to men of the strongest and most robust constitutions, allowing them no other food but herbs and such kind of unsubstantial nutriment, so that the nursing womens milk was desiccated and so dried up, and the young infants all perished, and females being separated from and debarred cohabitation with men, there was no proliferation or raising up issue among them. The men died in mines, hunger starved and oppressed with labor, and the women perished in the fields, harassed and broken with the same evils and calamities. The numerous inhabitants of this Island were exterminated and dwindled away to nothing by such consumptions and this was their end. They were compelled to carry eighty or a hundred pound weight for the distance of one to two hundred miles, while carrying the Spaniards on their shoulders by carriage or hammock (the kind made of net-work by the Indians). The Spaniards used the Indians as beasts to carry the burdens and cumbersome baggage of their journeys, so much so that many of the Indians backs and shoulders were deeply marked with scourges and stripes. As to the slashes made by the whips, stave's, cuffs and boxes, together with maledictions and curses and a thousand of such torments they suffered, all during the fatigue of their laborious journeys, that would require more time and paper to describe them, and when I were to finish you would be so horrified and consternated.

We must remember that the destruction of these Isles and Provinces began only after the Serene Queen Isabella died, about the year 1504, since before that very few of the Provinces were oppressed with unjust wars and violated with devastation, and those that were were concealed from the Queens knowledge (whom I hope God has crowned with Eternal Glory), since all knew of her fervent and wonderful zeal, almost divine desires, for the salvation and preservation of these people and these that we having seen with our eyes and felt with our hands, cannot easily be forgotten.

Here is a rule to learn, the Spaniards who landed on the coasts of American, exercised the same cruelties, slaughters, tyrannies and detestable oppressions on the most innocent Indian Nation, diverting themselves with delights in new sorts of torment, did in time improve in barbarism and cruelty; and the omnipotent suffered a more desperate and dangerous lapse into a immoral state.

Of the Isles of St. John and Jamaica

In the year 1509, the Spaniards sailed to the Islands of St. John and Jamaica with the same purpose and design they proposed to themselves in the Isle of Hispaniola, to perpetrate innumerable robberies and villainies as before; though here they added unheard of cruelties by murdering, burning, roasting and exposing men to be torn to pieces by Dogs; and finally by afflicting and harassing them with unexampled oppressions and torments in the mines, they depopulated the country of its innocent inhabitants.

These two Isles containing six hundred thousand at least, though at this day there are maybe two hundred men to be found in either of them, the remainder perishing without the knowledge of Christian faith or Sacrament.

Of the Isle of Cuba

In the year of our Lord 1511 they passed over to Cuba, which is as big in length as there is distance between Valledolid and Rome, with large, stately and very populated Provinces, against whom they proceeded with no more humanity and clemency, or indeed in fact with greater savageness and brutality. Several memorable transactions worthy of observation, passed in this Island. A man named Hathney, who not long before fled Hispaniola to Cuba for refuge from death, or captivity; and understanding by certain Indians that the Spaniards intended to steer their course his way, made this speech to all his people assembled together:

"You are not ignorant that there is a rumor spread abroad among us of the Spaniards arrival, and are sensible by woeful experience how such and such (naming them) and Haiti (so they term Hispaniola in their own language) with their inhabitants have been treated by them, that they design to visit us with equal intentions of committing such acts as they have been guilty of. But do you not know the cause and reason of their coming? We are altogether ignorant of it, they replied, but sufficiently satisfied that they are cruelly and wickedly inclined: Then thus they adore a certain covetous deity, whose cravings are not to be satisfied by a few moderate offerings, but they may answer his adoration and worship, demand many unreasonable things of us, and use their utmost endeavors to subjugate and afterwards murder us." Then taking up a casket near at hand, full of gold and gems, he proceeded in this manner: "This is the Spaniards God, and in honor of him if you think well of it, let us celebrate our Arcytos (which are certain kinds of dances); and by this means his deity being appeased, he will impose his commands on the Spaniards that they shall not for the future molest us!" Unanimously, with one consent, in a loud tone made this reply "Well said, Well said", and thus they continued skipping and dancing before this casket, without intermission, till they were quite tired and grown weary: Then the Noble Hathney re-assuming his discourse said: "If we worship this deity, till ye be ravished from us, we shall be destroyed, therefore I judge it convenient, upon mature deliberation, that we cast it into the river". This advice was approved of by all without opposition, and the casket was thrown in to the river.

When the Spaniards first touched this Island, Hathney, who was thoroughly acquainted with them, did avoid and shun them as much as he could and defended himself by force of arms, wherever he met with them, but when he was taken he was burnt alive, for fleeing from them and endeavoring to secure his life with out those who's only thirst was after the blood of himself and his own people.

Now being bound to the post for his execution, a certain Holy Monk of the Franciscan Order, discussed God and the Articles of our faith with him, which he never heard of before and which might be satisfactory and advantageous to him, considering the small time allowed him by the executioner, promising him eternal glory and repose, if he truly believed them or other wise everlasting torments. Hathney had been silently pensive sometime after the discussion, then asked the Monk whether the Spaniards also were admitted into Heaven. The Monk answered that the Gates of Heaven were open to all that were good and Godly. To this Hathney replied without further consideration, that he would rather go to Hell than Heaven, for fear he would cohabit in the same place as the sanguinary and bloody Nation since this is the God and the Holy Catholic faith that is praised and reverenced by the practices of the Spaniards in America.

Once, the citizens of a famous city, ten miles from our place of residence, came to meet us with a great entourage, to render their visit more honorable, bringing with them delicious provisions and wonderful dainties, with as much fish as they could possibly procure, distributing them among us; when all of a sudden, some wicked devil possessing the minds of the Spaniards, agitated them with great fury, that I being present, and without the least pretense or reason offered, they killed in cold blood above three thousand men, women and children promiscuously. These inhumanities and barbarisms were committed in my sight, and I will never forget them.

Some time after, I dispatched messengers to all the rulers of the Province of Havana, that they should by no means be terrified or seek refuge by absence and flight, but to meet us. I would make sure (for they understood my authority) that they should not receive the least of injuries; for the whole Country was extremely afflicted at the evils and mischiefs already perpetrated, and this I did with the advice of their Captain. As soon as we approached the Province, twenty two Noblemen came to greet us, and the Captain, who would have burned them to death for allegedly being against us even though they had no means to, had much difficulty doing so and that is how I snatched them out of the fire.

The Cubans, being reduced to the same bondage and misery as the Hispanics, seeing themselves perish and die without any amends, fled to the mountains for shelter. But there were those who chose to end their days and calamities by hanging themselves and their family. By the ferocity of one Spanish Tyrant (whom I knew), more than two hundred hung themselves by their own accord.

A certain person on this Isle constituted such a royal power, that the three hundred Indians that happened to fall in his share, after three months, through excessive labor, one hundred and sixty died. Some time after that only a tenth remained alive, namely thirty, but when that number was doubled they still perished in the same rate, and all those that were bestowed on him lost their lives, until he paid his last debt to nature and the Devil.

In the three or four months of my presence here, over six thousand children were murdered because they had lost their parents, who labored in the mines; but I have witnessed many other stupendous villainies.

And still they consulted on how to persecute those that hid in the mountains, and were miserably massacred, so consequently this Isle became desolate, which I saw not long after, and a dreadful and deplorable sight to behold since it depopulated and laid to waste, like a desert.

Of the Continent

In the year 1514, a certain unhappy Governor landed on the Continent, a most bloody Tyrant, destitute of all mercy and prudence, the instrument of God's wrath, with a resolution to populate these parts with Spaniards; and although some Tyrants had been here before him and their cruelty killed them by several ways of slaughter, even though they got no farther than the sea coast - where they committed prodigious thefts and robberies, this person exceeded all that ever happened in other Islands, though deplorable and profligate Villains. He did not only ravage and depopulate the Sea-Coast, but buried the largest Regions and most ample Kingdoms in their own ruins, sending thousands to Hell by his Butcheries. He made incursions in those Countries that are included in the Territories of Darien (Panama) and the Provinces of Nicaragua, where are near five hundred miles of the most fertile land in the world, and the most opulent for gold of all the Regions discovered yet. Although Spain has been sufficiently furnished with the purest gold, the said gold has been mined at the said countries by the Indians where they have perished (as we said).

This Ruler, with his accomplices, found out new inventions to rack, torment, force and extort gold from the Indians. One of his Captains in a certain excursion undertaken by the Command of his Governor to make Depredations, destroyed forty thousand people by exposing them to the edge of the sword, fire, dogs and other torments; all in the presence of a Man of the Order of St. Francis, Franciskus De S. Romano.

Great and Injurious was the blindness of those presided over the Indians. As to the Conversion and Salvation of this People: they denied in effect what was declared with their tongue but contradicted with their heart; for it came to pass that the Indians should be commanded on the penalty of a bloody war, death and perpetual bondage, to embrace the Christian faith, and submit to the obedience of the Spanish King. This is as if the Son of God, who suffered Death for the redemption of all Mankind, had enacted a Law by saying: "Go and teach all Nations that Infidels, living peaceably and quietly in their Native Country, should be imposed upon with pain of confiscation of all their chattels, lands, liberty, wives, children and death itself, without any need for them to confess and acknowledge the true God, and subject themselves to a King, whom they never saw, or heard mentioned of before"; and whose Messengers took these words in seriousness by acting in inhumane and cruel ways. This, of course, is an elegant and absurd way of proceeding and merits nothing but scandal, derision and even hell. Now suppose this Notorious and Profligate Governor was made to see the execution of these edicts performed, for they were repugnant both to Law and Equity; yet he commanded (or they who were to see the Execution, did it of their own Heads without Authority) that any place they fancied that was rich with gold, they had the right to rob the Indians living in their cities and houses as if it weren't an ill act. These wicked Spaniards proclaimed these edicts, in this manner, like thieves, any where that pleased them: "You, Cacics and Indians of this Continent, the Inhabitants of such a Place

29

(which they named); We declare or be it known to you all, that there is but one God, one hope, and one King of Castile, who is Lord of these Countries; appear forth without delay, and take the oath of Allegiance to the Spanish King, as his Vassals".

Right before dawn, at about three in the morning, these poor innocents overwhelmed with heavy Sleep, ran violently from the fire set to their hovels which were all thatched, so that without notice, burnt men, women and children; killed whom they pleased on the spot. But those they preserved as Captives, were compelled through torments, to confess where they had hid the gold. When they found little or none at their houses, those who lived, being first stigmatized, were made Slaves; yet after the fire extinguished, they came hastily in quest of the gold. This is how the Wicked Man, devoted to all the Infernal Furies, behaved himself with the assistance of profligate Christians, whom he had enlisted between the 14th to the 21st or 22nd year. Together with his domestic servants and followers, from whom he received as many portions, besides what he had from his slaves in gold, pearls and jewels, as the Chief Governor was allowed and all that were constituted to execute any kind of Kingly Office followed in the same footsteps. Every one sending as many of his servants as he could spare, to share in the spoil. Even those called Bishops did the same when at the very time (as I conjecture) the Spaniards robbed this Kingdom of over a million Castillian Crowns. Though in these years over eight hundred thousand men were killed, the tyrants who followed (until the year 1533) murdered the remaining inhabitants.

Among all those flagellation Acts committed by this Governor while he ruled this Kingdom, or by his Consent and Permission, this must by no means be omitted: A certain Casic, bestowing on him a Gift, voluntarily, or which is more probably induced by Fear, of the weight of Nine Thousand Crowns, left the Spaniards unsatisfied with the Sum of Money, seized him and fixed him to a pole; they extended his feet near the fire and demanded a larger sum. Overcome with torments the Casic procured three thousand more and presented them. This made the Spaniards furious adding new torments since he would not confer more (which was because he could not), that they exposed him to their torments so long that the heat made the marrow gush out of the soles of his feet, killing him. This is how they murdered many Lords and Nobles to extort the gold from them.

Once a party of one hundred Spaniards making an excursion, arrived at a mountain, and found the hiding place of those running from them. As they saw them, the Spaniards immediately slain all they could met, securing seventy or eighty married women and even virgins captive, when a great number of Indians with a fervent desire of recovering their wives and daughters appeared in arms against the Spaniards, who were unwilling to relinquish their prey and so they had slain the women.   The Indians, through grief, smiting their Breasts, brake out into these Exclamations: "O perverse Generation of men! O Cruel Spaniards! What do you Murder *las Iras*?" (In their Language they call Women by the Name of *las Iras* as if they had said: To slay Women is an Act of bloody minded men, worse than Brutes and Wild Beasts).

There was the House of a Powerful Dictator situated about ten or fifteen miles from Panama, whose name was Paris, very Rich in gold; the Spaniards visited him and they were courteously received. He out of his own accord, presented them with a gift of fifteen thousand Crowns. The Captain was of the opinion, as well as the rest of the Spaniards, that he who gives that quantity of money was the master of a great treasure. The Spaniards pretended to depart only to return after four nights, entering the city by surprise, putting it to flames with many of its citizens, and robbed them of fifty or sixty thousand crowns. The Dictator escaped together with as great number of men as he could gather at that instant, and after three-four days elapsed pursued the Spaniards (who stole an extra hundred and thirty-forty thousand crowns), recovering all his gold and killing fifty Spaniards as the remainder were wounded and fled. Few days past and the Spaniards returned, overthrowing the Casic and all his forces, and those who outlived the battle, to their great misfortune, became slaves.

Of the Province of Nicaragua

The said Tyrant An. Dom. 1522. proceeded farther, unfortunately, to the subjugation of conquest of this Province. In truth, no one can satisfactorily tell about the birthrate, climate or multitude of inhabitants of Nicaragua, which was almost infinite and admirable; for this region contained some Cities that were four miles long and abundance agriculture (which was the cause of such a concourse of people). The People of this place, because the Country was level and plain, destitute of mountains and so very delightful and pleasant, that they could not leave it without great grief, and much dissatisfaction, they were therefore tormented with great vexations and persecutions, forced to bear the Spanish tyranny and servitude, with as much patience as they could master; even peaceable and meek spirited. This Tyrant in his cruelty, did afflict this nation (whose advice he made use of in destroying the other Kingdoms) with such and so many great damages, slaughters, injustice, slaver, and barbarism that a tongue, though of iron, could not express them all fully. He sent into the Province (which is larger than the County of Russia) fifty Horsemen, who murdered all the people, sparing none for no reason: for example, if they did not come to them with all possible speed, when called and bring the imposed *burthen* of *Mahid* (which signifies Corn in their Dialect) or if they did not bring the number of Indians required to his own and the service or rather servitude of his associates. And since the country had no mountains, no Person was able to withstand the hellish fury of their horses.

He commanded the Spaniards to make excursions, that is, to rob other Provinces, permitting and granting these thieving rogues leave to take away by force as many of these peaceable people as they could, who being ironed (that they might not sink under the burden of sixty or eighty pound weight) frequently found their death and out of four thousand people only six returned. If any of them chanced to faint, being tired with over-weight burdens or through great hunger and thirst should be seized with an outburst, if too much debility and weakness made them not able to take off their fetters quick enough, they were beheaded, so the head fell one way and the body another. The Indians, seeing the Spaniards preparing for such Journeys, knowing very well that few or none returned home alive, just upon their setting out with sighs and tears, burst out into these or the like expressions: "Those were journeys, which we traveled frequently in the service of Christians, and in some tract of time we returned to our habitations, wives and children: But now there being no hope of a return, we are for ever deprived of their sight and conversation".

That same President would dissipate or disperse the Indians at his own pleasure, to the end (as it was reported) he might violently force the Indians away as he pleased and dispose of them to others; so that for a whole year there was no sowing and planting. When the Spaniards wanted bread, by force they plundered the Indians of the whole stock of corn that was planted to support their families, and in this indirect way over thirty thousand perished with hunger. It is sad that at the end, mothers suppressed with insufferable hunger, deprived their own children of their lives to preserve their own.

In this Province also they brought many to an untimely end, loading their shoulders with heavy planks and pieces of Timer, which they were compelled to carry to a haven forty miles away in order to build their ships; sending them this way to the mountains to find out honey and wax, where they were devoured by tigers; alas they loaded women impregnated with burdens fit for beasts.

But no greater pest was there that could unpeople this Province, than the license granted the Spaniards by this Governor, to demand Captives from the inhabitants of this Region; for after four or five months, or as often as the Governor demanded them to appear, they delivered fifty servants, while the Spaniards terrified them by telling them that if they did not obey by answering their unreasonable demands, they should be burnt alive or baited to death by dogs. Now the Indians have few servants, so if the Casic has three or four in his retinue they were saved; but after they took the orphans, the Spaniards took one son from parents who had two and two from those who had three and so forth, for the Lord of the region satisfied the desires of the Tyrant, not without the effusion of tears and groans of the People, who (as it seems) were very careful of their children. This being frequently repeated between the year 1523 and 1533, the Kingdom lost all their inhabitants, for in six or seven years time there were constantly five or six ships made ready to be freighted with Indians that were sold in the Regions of Panama and Perusium, where they all died; for it is by daily experience proved and known, that the Indians when transported out of their Native Country into another soon died, because they were withheld food, and the task imposed on them in no way diminished, they being only bought for Labor. By this means, there have been taken out of this province over five hundred thousand Inhabitants, who before were freemen and made Slaves. In the Wars made on them, the horrid bondage, they were reduced to fifty or sixty thousand and more perished, and to this day very many still are destroyed. Now all these slaughters have been committed in Fourteen years inclusively, possibly in this Province of Nicaragua there remains four or five thousand men who are put to death by ordinary and personal oppressions, whereas (according to what is said already) it did exceed other Countries of the World in multitude of People.

Of new Spain

New Spain was discovered in 1517 and in the detection there was no first or second Attempt, but all were exposed to slaughter. The year ensuing those Spaniards (who call themselves Christians) came to rob, kill and slay, though they pretend they undertook this voyage to people the country. From that year to the present, 1542 the injustice, violence and tyranny of the Spaniards came to the highest degree of extremity. They shook hands with and bid adieu to all fear of God and King, unmindful of themselves in this sad and deplorable condition, for the destructions, cruelties, butcheries, devastations, the demolishing of Cities, depredations, etc. which they perpetrated in so many and such ample Kingdoms, are such and so great and strike the minds of men with so great horror, that all we have related before are inconsiderable comparatively to those which have been acted from the year 1518 to 1542, and to this very month of September that we now live to see the most heavy, grievous and detestable things are committed, that the Rule we laid down before as a maxim might be indubitably verify to wit, that from the start they ran headlong from bad to worse and were overcome in their diabolical acts and wickedness only by themselves.

From the first entrance of the Spaniards into New Spain, which happened on the 18th day of April in the said month of the year 1518 to 1530, the space of ten whole years, there was no end or period put to the destruction and slaughters committed by the merciless hands of the blood-thirsty Spaniard in the Continent, or space of 450 Miles round about Mexico, and the adjacent or neighboring parts, which might contain four or five spacious Kingdoms, that neither for magnitude or fertility would give

35

Spain her self the pre-eminence. This entire Region was more populous then Toledo, Sevil, Valedolid, Saragoza and Faventia; and there is not at this day in all of them as many people, nor when they flourished in their greatest height and splendor was there such a number, as inhabited that Region, which embraced which then was four hundred and eighty Miles. Within these twelve years, the Spaniards have destroyed in the Continent, by spears, fire and sword over four million men, women and children in their conquests (for under that word they mask their Cruel Actions). Rather those of the Turk himself, which report them tending to the ruin of the Catholic Cause, together with their invasions and unjust wars, contrary to the Divine and Human Laws; their number, of those who perished by them is even more than the Egyptian bondage.

There is no language, art or human knowledge that can recite the horrid impieties, which these capital enemies to government and all mankind have been guilty of at several times and in several nations; nor can the circumstantial aggravations of some of their wicked acts be unfolded or displayed by any manner of industry, time or writing, yet I will say that somewhat of every individual particular thing, which this protestation and oath, that I conceive I am not able to comprehend one of a Thousand.

Of New Spain in Particular

Among other slaughters, they also perpetrated in the spacious City of Cholula, which consisted of thirty thousand families, all of them the rulers of that Region and neighboring places. First the Priests with their High Priest went to meet the Spaniards in Pomp and State, and to the end they gave them a more reverential and honorable reception appointing them as such, so that they might, being entertained in the apartments of the most powerful and principal Noblemen, stay in the city. The Spaniards discussed how they will further their slaughters that they might fill every corner of the Region with their cruelties and wicked deeds with terror and consternation; for this is how they began their ruling in all the countries, by immediately committing some notorious butchery, which made the innocent sheep tremble for fear. To this purpose they sent for the governors and Nobles of the cities they subjected, together with their supreme Governor, to appear before them and no sooner did they congregate,the Spaniards detained them before they had time to cry for help. They demanded they bring six thousand Indians to carry their carriage of baggage; no sooner did they come, the Spaniards clasped them into their yard, there to enclose them.

It was a thing worthy of pity and compassion to see the wretched people in the condition they were in, prepared to receive the burdens laid on them by the Spaniards. They came to them naked, their Privies only veiled, their Shoulders laden with food; only covered with a Net, they laid themselves quietly on the ground, and shrinking in their bodies like poor wretches, killed themselves. Being all gathered together in their yards, some of the armed Spaniards held the doors to drive them away if they attempted to bolt and others with lances and swords butchered the innocents so that not one of them escaped, though two or three days after, those who hid themselves among the dead bodies, being all over sprinkled with blood and gore, presented themselves to the Spaniards, imploring their mercy and the prolongation of their lives with tears in their eyes and all imaginable submission, yet they, not in the least moved with pity or compassion, tore them in pieces. But all the Chief Governors who were over one hundred in number, were kept bound, only to be burnt alive. The King of the country escaped along with thirty or forty gentlemen, to a Temple (called in their Tongue *Quu*) which he made use of as a Castle or place of defense, and there defended himself for a great part of the day, but the Spaniards, who suffer none, escaped out of their clutches, especially Soldiers, setting fire to the Temple, burning all those that were there enclosed, and broke out into these dying words and exclamations: "O profligate men, what injury have we done you to occasion our death! Go, go to Mexico, where our supreme Lord Montencuma will revenge our cause upon your persons".

It is reported that while the Spaniards were engaged in this tragedy, destroying six or seven thousand men, that their Commander with great rejoicing sang this following song; "*Mira Nero de Tarpeia, Roma como se ardia, Gritos de Ninos y Vieyot, y el de nadase dolia*".

"From the Tarpian still Nero espies

Rome all in Flames with unrelenting Eyes,

And hears of young and old the dreadful Cries."

They also committed a very great Butchery in the City Tepeara, which was larger and better housed than the former; and here they massacred an incredible number at the point of the Sword.

Setting sail from Cholula, they steered their course to Mexico, whose King sent his Nobles and Peers with abundance of presents to meet them on the way, portraying to them how grateful their arrival was and acceptable to him: but when they came to a steep Hill, his brother went forward to meet them, accompanied with many Noblemen who brought them many gifts in gold, silver, and Robes embroidered with gold and at their entrance into the City, the King himself carried in a golden litter, together (with the whole Court) attended them to the Palace prepared for their reception; and that very day as I was informed by some persons, then and there present by a grand piece of treachery, they took the very great King Montencuma, never so much as dreaming of any such surprise, and put him into the custody of eighty Soldiers and clasping his legs with irons; even though I am writing this lightly, one act I will merit your observation: When the Captain arrived at the Haven, to fight with a Spanish Officer who made war against him, and left another with a hundred Soldiers, more or less, as a Guard to King Montencuma, they thought that their acts will be better remembered if the dread of their cruelty might be more and more apprehended, and greatly increased.

In the interim, all the nobles of the city thought of nothing else but of ways to console the spirit of their Captive King, with a variety of diversions. Among them revelings and dances which they celebrated in all streets and highways at night and they in their idiot term *Mirotes*; to these masquerades and jigs they usually go with all their riches, costly vestments and robes, together with any thing that is precious and glorious, being wholly addicted to this humor, nor is there any greater token among them then this of their extraordinary exultation and rejoicing. The Nobles in like manner, and Princes of the Blood Royal, every one according to his degree, exercised these Masques and Dances, in some place adjoining to the House where their King and Lord was detained Prisoner. Now not far from the Palace, about 2000 Young Noblemen who were the issue of the greatest Potentates of the Kingdom, and indeed the flower of the whole Nobility of King Montencuma, were visited by the Spanish Captain with some soldiers, and sent others to the rest of the places in the City where these Revelings were kept, under pretense only of being spectators of the solemnity. Now the Captain had commanded, that at a certain hour appointed, they should fall upon these Revelers, and he himself approaching the Indians very busy dancing, said: "San Jago (that is St. James) Let us rush in upon them", which was no sooner heard, and they all began with their naked Swords in hand to pierce their tender and naked bodies, and spill their generous and Noble blood, till not one of them was left alive on the place, and the rest following his example in other parts, (to their inexpressible stupefaction and grief) seized on all these Provinces. The inhabitants will never stop their celebrations of lamentation and singing, the calamity and ruin of the ancient nobility of their whole kingdom, which was their pride and glory, even while their kind lay in inferno.

The Indians, seeing this not to be exampled cruelty and iniquity executed against such a number of guiltless people, and bearing with incredible patience the unjust imprisonment of their King from whom they had an absolute Command not to take up arms against the Spaniard, the whole City was suddenly up in arms fell on the Spaniards and wounded many of them, the rest hardly escaping; but they, presenting the point of a sword to the Kings Breast, threatened him with death unless he out of the Window commanded them to desist; but the Indians, for the present, disobeying the Kings Mandate, proceeded to the election of a Generalissimo, or Commander in Chief over all their Forces; and because the Captain, who went to the Port returned victor and brought away a far greater number of Spaniards then he took along with him, there was a cessation of arms for three or four days, till he re-entered the City, then the Indians having gathered together and made up a great army, fought so long and so strenuously that the Spaniards despairing of their safety, called a Council of war and resolved to retreat in the dead time of night. So they drew their forces out of the City. When this knowledge hit the Indians, they destroyed a great number retreating on the Bridges made over their lakes in this just and Holy War, for the causes above-mentioned, deserving the approbation of every upright Judge. But afterward, the Spaniards having recruited and got together, they resolved to take the City and carried it out where most detestable butcheries were acted, a vast number of the people slain, and their Rulers perished in the flames.

All these horrid murders were committed in Mexico and other Cities ten, fifteen and twenty miles away. This same tyranny and plague in the abstract, proceeded to infest and lay desolate

Panuco; a Region abounding with inhabitants even to admiration, nor were the slaughters there perpetrated less stupendous and wonderful. In the same manner, they utterly laid waste the Provinces of Futepeca, Ipilcingonium and Columbia, every one of them being as large as the Kingdoms of Leon, and Castile. It would be very difficult or rather impossible to relate the cruelties and destruction there made and committed, and prove very nauseous and offensive to the reader.

To observe, that they entered upon these dominions and laid waste the Indian Territories, so populous, that it would have rejoiced the hearts of all true Christians to see their number upon no other title or pretense, but only to enslave them; for at their first arrival they compelled them to swear an oath of obedience and fealty to the King of Spain, and if they did not they menace them with death and vassalage; and they who did appear to satisfy the inequitable Mandate and submit to the will and pleasure of such unjust and cruel men, were declared rebels and accused of that crime before our Lord the King. The blindness and ignorance of those who ruled over the Indians, darkened their understanding and apprehension, the known and incontrovertible maxim in Law, that no man can be called a rebel who is not first proved to be a subject. I omit the injuries and prejudice they do to the King himself when they spoil and ravage his Kingdoms. And as much as in them lies, diminish and impair all his right and title to the Indians, in plain English, invalidate and make it null and void. These are the worthy services which the Spaniards do for our Kings in those Countries, by the unjust and colorful pretenses that were said.

This Tyrant, upon the same pretext, sent two other Captains who exceeded him in impiety and cruelty (if possible), to the most flourishing and Fertile (in Fruits and men) Kingdoms of Guatemala, situated Southward, who had also received orders to go to the Kingdoms of Naco, Honduras and Guaymura, upon the

North, and border with Mexico, three hundred miles together. The one was sent by Land and the other by Sea, and both well furnished with Horse and Foot.

This I declare is true, that the outrages committed by these two, particularly by him that went to Guatemala (for the other not long after his departure died a violent death) would fill an entire volume, and when completed he so crowded with slaughters, injuries, butcheries and inhuman desolations, so horrid and detestable as would Ague-shake the present as well as future ages with terror.

He that put out to sea, vexed all the transportation with his cruel incursions. Some inhabitants of the Kingdom of Yucatan which is seated in the way to the Kingdoms of Naco and Naymura, to which places he steered his course, came to meet him with many presents and gifts, and as soon as he approached, they sent his Captains with a party of Soldiers to murder the people who committed great spoils and made cruel slaughters among them; and in particular a seditious and rebellious Officer who with three hundred soldiers entered Guatemala, and there, firing at the Cities and murdering all the inhabitants, violently depriving them of all their goods, which he did, in a hundred and twenty mile radius. At the end, if his companions should follow them, they might find the country laid waste and destroyed by the Indians, in revenge for the damage they had received by him and his forces which happened accordingly: for the Chief Commander whose order the above said Captain had disobeyed and so became a rebel to him, was slain.

But many other bloody Tyrants succeeded him, who from the year 1524 to 1535, depopulated the desert of the Provinces of Naco and Honduras (as well as other places), which were looked upon as the Paradise of delights, and better populated than other Regions; insomuch that within the these eleven years, over two million men were killed in those countries and now there are hardly remain two thousand, who daily die by the severity of their slavery.

But to return to that great Tyrant who outdid the former in cruelty (as hinted above) and is equal to those that tyrannize there at present, who traveled to Guatemala; he from the Provinces adjoining to Mexico, which according to his prosecuted journey (as he himself writes and testifies with his own hand in Letters to the Prince of Tyrants) are four hundred miles away from Guatemala, made it his urgent and daily business to procure ruin and destruction by slaughter, fire and depopulation, compelling all to submit to the Spanish King, whom they looked upon to be more unjust and cruel than his inhumane and bloodthirsty Ministers.

Of the Kingdom and Province of Guatemala

When the Tyrant first entered Guatemala, he commanded prodigious slaughters. As he entered there were parties for him attended by the Chief Lord and many Nobles of the City of Ultlatana, the capital of the whole Kingdom, together with trumpets, drums and great exultation, bringing all sorts of food in great abundance and things that he was in need of. That night, the Spaniards slept outside the City, for they feared their security was in danger there. The next day he commanded the Lord and many of his Peers to come before him, and requested a certain quantity of gold; to which the Indians replied that they cannot satisfy his demands (and indeed the region had no gold mines), and with that they were all burnt alive with no other crime laid to their charge. The rest of the Nobles belonging to other Provinces, when hearing of their Chief Lords death for the sole reason of not having gold, fled to the mountains (their usual refuge) knowing that their future would be the same for that same reason, commanding their subjects to obey the Spaniards, as Lords, but not to tell of their flight and its destination. The Indians obeyed

43

their Lords only to hear that they would be put to death if they would not tell of their Lords hiding place. The Indians answered that they were ignorant of the matter, but they, their wives and children will serve them and they may deal with them as they pleased. And the Spaniards did – they killed them all by swords , the men, woman and children when they thought they were safe and free of danger. A large village they destroyed in two hours, sparing none, with out mercy.

The Indians, perceiving that this barbarous and hard-hearted people will not be pacified with humility, large gifts or unexampled patience, but were butchered without any cause, seriously considered rebelling and fighting for their lives and liberty. They conceived that it was far better (since death to them was a necessary evil) to be killed when armed by taking revenge of the enemy, then be murdered by them without satisfaction. But when they realized their wants of arms, their nakedness and debility and that they were incapable of handling a horse so as to defeat such a furious adversary, recollecting themselves, they contrived this strategy to dig ditches and holes in the highway so that their horses might fall in their passage, and putting, purposely sharp and burnt posts and covering them with loose dirt, so as not to be seen by their riders. The horses fell twice or thrice into those holes, but afterward the Spaniards took this course to prevent them for the future; and made this a Law, that as many of the Indians of what age or sex that were taken, should be cast into these ditches that they had made. They threw into them women with child and as many aged men as they could till they were filled to capacity with carcasses. It was a sight deserving commiseration, to see women and children gaunt or run through with these posts, some were taken off by spears and swords and the remainder exposed to hungry dogs kept short of food for that purpose, to be devoured by them and torn in pieces. They burnt a potent Nobleman in a very great fire, saying, that he was the more honored by this kind of death. All which butcheries continued seven years, from 1524 to 1531. I leave the reader to judge how many might be massacred during that time.

Among the innumerable factitious acts done by this Tyrant and his partners (for they were as barbarous as their principal) in this Kingdom, this also occurs worthy of an afterism in the margin: In the Province of Cuzcatan in which S. Saviour's City is situated, a country with a seacoast that extends forty or fifty miles in length, Miles, as also in the very City of Cuzcatan, the Metropolis of the whole Province, he was entertained with great applause: for about twenty or thirty thousand Indians brought with them hens and other necessary provisions, expecting this coming. He, accepting their gifts, commended every single Spaniard to make choice of as many of these people, as he had a mind to, that during their stay there, they might use them as Servants, and forced to undergo the most submissive offices they should impose on them. Every one culled out a hundred, or fifty, according as he thought convenient for his peculiar service, and these wretched Indians did serve the Spaniards with their utmost strength and endeavor; so that there could be nothing wanting in them but adoration. In the mean time this Captain required a great sum of gold from their Lords (for that was the load-stone that attracted them there) who answered, they were content to deliver him up all the gold they had in possession; and the Indians gathered a great number of spears gilded with Orichalcum (which had the appearance of gold, and in truth some gold in them intermixed) and they were presented to him. The Captain ordered them to be touched and when he found them to be Orichalcum or mixed metal, he ordered the Spaniards as follows:"Let that Nation that is without gold be accursed to the Pit of Hell. Let every Man detain those Servants he elected, let them be clasped in irons, and stigmatized with the brand of Slavery" this was accordingly done, for they were all burnt, who did no escape with the King's Mark. I my self saw the impression made on the Son of the Chiefest Person in the City. Those that escaped, with other

45

Indians, engaged the Spaniards by force of arms, but with such ill success, that abundance of them lost their lives in the attempt. After this, they returned to Guatemala, where they built a City, which God in his Judgment leveled in its own ashes with three deluges, the first of water, the Second of earth and third of stones, as big as half a score Oxen, all concurring at one and the same time. Now all being slain who were capable of bearing arms against them, the rest were enslaved, paying so much per head for men and women as a ransom; for they use no other servitude here, and then they were sent into Pecusium to be sold, by which means together with their slaughters committed upon the Inhabitants, they destroyed and made a desert of this Kingdom, which contains a hundred miles radius; and with his associates and brethren in wickedness, four millions at least in fifteen or sixteen years, that is from 1524 to 1540 were murdered, and daily continues destroying the small residue of that People with his cruelties and brutishness.

It was the usual custom of this Tyrant, when he made war with any City or Province, to take along with him as many of those Indians he had subjugated as he could, that they might fight with their countrymen; and when he had in his army twenty or sometimes thirty thousand of them and could not afford them sustenance, he permitted them to feed on the flesh of other Indians taken prisoners in war; and so kept a shambles of Man's flesh in his army, suffered children to be killed and roasted before his face. They butchered the men's feet and hands only; for these members were accounted by them dainties, most delicious Food.

He as the Death of many by the intolerable labor of carrying ships by land, causing them to transport those vessels with anchors of a vast weight from the septentrional to the Mediterranean Sea, which are one hundred and thirty miles distant; which had an abundance of guns of the largest fort, which they carried on their bare, naked shoulders, so that oppressed with many ponderous burdens, (I say no more than what I saw) they dyed by the way. He separated and divided families, forcing married men from their wives, and maids from their parents, which he bestowed upon his mariners and soldiers, to gratify their burning lust. All his ships he freighted with Indians, where hunger and thirst discharged them of their servitude and his cruelty by a welcome death. He had two companies of soldiers who tore them in pieces, like thunder from heaven speedily. O how many parents has he robbed of their children, how many wives of their husbands and children of their parents? How many adulteries, rapes and what libidinous acts has he been guilty of? How many has he enslaved and oppressed with insufferable anguish and unspeakable calamities? How many tears, sighs and groans has he occasioned? To how many has he been the author of desolation during their peregrination in this and of damnation in the World to come, not only to Indians, whose number is numberless, but even to Spaniards themselves, by whose help and assistance he committed such detestable butcheries and flagitious crimes? I supplicate Almighty God, that he would please to have mercy on his soul and require no other satisfaction than the violent death, which turned him out of this World.

All which I affirm of all their other Transactions and passages in America

A farther Discourse of New Spain: Some Account of Panuco and Xalisco

After the perpetration of all the cruelties rehearsed in New Spain and other places, there came another rabid and cruel Tyrant to Panuco, who acted the part of a bloody tragedian as well as the rest, and sent away many ships loaded with these barbarians to be sold for slaves, made this Province almost a wilderness and which deplored eight hundred Indians, that had rational souls were given in exchange for a burthen-bearing-beast, a mule or camel. Well, he was made Governor of the City of Mexico and all New Spain, and with him many other Tyrants had the office of Auditors bestowed upon them. Now, they had already made such a progress toward the desolation of this Region, that if the Franciscans had not vigorously opposed them and that by (the King's Council, the best and greatest encourager of virtue) it, had been prevented quickly, that which happened to Hispaniola in two years, had been the fate of Hispania nova, namely to be unpopulated, deferred and entombed in its own rules. A companion of this Governor employed eight thousand Indians in erecting a wall to enclose his garden, but they all died, having no supplies or wages from him to support themselves, at whose death he was not in the least concerned.

After the first Captain, before spoken of, had absolutely profligate and ruined the Panuconians, fifteen thousand perished by carrying their bag and baggage. At length, he arrived at the Province of Michoacan, which is forty miles journey from Mexico and as fertile and populated. The King to honor him in the encounter, with a many people, marched toward him, from whom he had received one thousand services and civilities very considerable, who gratefully requited him with captivity, because his fame was heard of abroad, that he was a most Opulent Prince in gold and silver; and to the end he might export from and purge him of his gold, he was crucified with torments after this manner; his body was extended, hands bound to a post and his feet put into a pair of stocks, they, all the while applying burning coals to his feet at a tormenting distance, where a boy attended, who by little and little sprinkled them with Oil, that his flesh might roast the better. Before him there stood a wicked fellow, presenting a bow to his breast charged with a mortal arrow, (if let fly) behind him, another with dogs held in with chains which he threatened to let loose at him, which if done, he would be torn to pieces in a moment; and with these kind of torments they racked him confess where he hid his treasures; till a Franciscan Monk came and delivered him from his torments, but not from death, for he departed this miserable life not long after. This was the severe fate of many Cacics and Indian Lords, who died with the same torments which they were exposed to by the Spaniards, in order to the engrossing of their gold and Sliver to themselves.

At this very time, a certain visitor of purses rather than souls happened to be here present, who (finding some Indian Idols which were hid; for they were no better instructed in the Knowledge of the true God by reason of the wicked documents and dealings of the Spaniards) detained grandees as slaves, till they had delivered him all their Idols, for he fancied they were made of gold or silver, but his expectation being frustrated, he chastised them with no less cruelty than injustice; and that he might not depart bubbled out of all his hopes, constrained them to redeem their Idols with money, that so they might, according to their custom, adore them. These are the fruits of the Spanish artifices and juggling tricks among the Indians, and thus they promoted the honor and worship of God.

This Tyrant from Michoacan arrives at Xalisco, a Country abounding with People very fruitful and the glory of the Indians in this respect, that it had some towns seven miles long; and among other barbarisms equal to what you have read, which they acted here, this is not to be forgotten: that women big with child, were burthened with the luggage of wicked Christians and being unable to go out their usual time, through extremity of toil and hunger, were necessitated to bring them forth in the highways, which was the death of many infants.

At a certain time a profligate Christian attempted to rape a maid, but the mother being present, resisted him and endeavoring to free her from his intended rape and the Spaniard, enraged, cut off her hand with a short sword and stabbed the virgin in several places, till she died, because she obstinately opposed and disappointed his inordinate appetite.

In this Kingdom of Xalisco (according to report) they burnt eight hundred towns to ashes, and for this reason the Indians, growing desperate, beholding the daily destruction of the remainders of their matchless cruelty, made an insurrection against the Spaniards, slew several of them justly and deservedly and afterward fled to the insensible rocks and mountains (yet more tender and kind than the stony-hearted enemy) for sanctuary; where they were miserably massacred by those Tyrants who succeeded, and there are now few or no inhabitants to be found. The Spaniards, being blinded with their lust for gold, deserted by God, and given over to a reprobate sense, not understanding (or at least not willing to do so) that the cause of the Indians is most just, as well by the Law of Nature, as the Divine and humane, they by force of arms, destroying them, hacking them in pieces and turning them out of their own confines and dominions, not considering how unjust those violences and tyrannies are, where they have afflicted these poor creatures, they still contrive to raise new wars against them. They don not conceive, that those victories they have obtained against those innocents to their ruin, are granted them by God himself, as if their unjust wars were promoted and managed by a just right and title to what they pretend; and with boasting joy, return thanks to God for their tyranny, in imitation of those tyrants and robbers, of whom the Prophet Zechariah part of the forth and fifth Verses: "Feed the

Sheep of the slaughter, whose Possessors slay them, and hold themselves not guilty, and they that sell them say, Blessed by the Lord, for ye are rich".

Of the Kingdom of Jucatan

A profane wretch, by his fabulous stories and relations to the King of Spain, was made perfect of the Kingdom of Jucatan, in the year of our Lord 1526; The other Tyrants, to this very day, have taken the same indirect measures to obtain offices and screw or wheedle themselves into public charges or employments, for this pretext and authority, they had the greater opportunity to commit theft and rape.

This Kingdom was very well populated, and both for climate and plenty of food and fruits, in which respect it is most fertile than Mexico, but mainly with honey and wax, it exceeds all the Indian countries that have been discovered at present. It is three hundred miles in radius. The inhabitants of this place excel all other Indians, either in polite or prudence or in leading a regular life and morality, truly deserving to be instructed in the knowledge of the true God. Here the Spaniards might have erected many fair cities and lived as it were in a garden of delights, if they had not, through covetousness, stupidity and weight of enormous crimes, rendered themselves unworthy of so great a benefit. This Tyrant, with three hundred men, began to make war with these innocent people, living peaceably at home and doing injury to none, which was the ruin of a great number of them. Now, because this Region affords no gold and if it did, the inhabitants would soon have wrought away their lives by hard working in the mines, that so he might accumulate gold by their bodies and souls, for which Christ was Crucified. In general, he made slaves of those whose lives he spared and sent away such ships as were driven by the wind of report, loaded with them, exchanging them for wine, oil, vinegar, salt pork, garments, pack horses and other commodities, which he thought most necessary and fit for his use. He proposed to them the choice of fifty virgins and she that was the fairest or best complexioned, he bartered for a small cask of wine, oil, vinegar or some inconsiderable quantity of salt pork, the same exchange he proffered of two or three hundred well-disposed young boys and one of them, who had the mind or presence of a Princes Son, was given up to them for a cheese and one hundred more for a horse. He continued his flagitious courses from 1526 to 1533 inclusively, till there was news of the wealth and opulence in the Region of Persia, where the Spaniards marched to, so for some time there was a cessation of this tyranny; but few days after, they returned and acted enormous crimes, robbed and imprisoned them and committed higher offenses against the God of Heaven that they haven't done, so that now these three hundred miles of land, so populated (as I said before) lies now uncultivated and almost deserted.

No solifidian can believe the particular narrations of their barbarism and cruelty in those Countries. I will only relate two or three stories which are fresh in my memory. The Spaniards used to trace the steps of the Indians, both men and women, with cursed currs, furious dogs; an Indian woman that was sick happened to be in the way in sight, who perceiving that she was not able to avoid being torn in pieces by the dogs, takes a cord that she had and hangs her self upon a beam, tying her child (which she unfortunately had with her) to her foot; and no sooner had she done, yet the dogs were at her, tearing the child, but a priest coming that way baptized it before quite dead.

When the Spaniards left this Kingdom, one of them invited the Son of some Indian governor of a City or Province, to go along with him, who told him he would not leave or desert his Native country, whereupon he threatened to cut off his ears, if he refused to follow him: but the youth persisting resolutely, that he would continue in the place of his Nativity, he drawing his sword cut off each ear, notwithstanding which he persevered in his first opinion and then as if he had only pinched him, smilingly cut off his nose and lips. This rogue did lasciviously boast before a priest and as if he had merited the greatest applause, commended himself to the very heavens, saying, "He had made it his chief Trade or Business to impregnate Indian Women, that when they were sold afterward, he might gain the more Money by them."

In this Kingdom or (I'm certain) in some Province of New Spain, a Spaniard hunting and intent on his game, fancied that his beagles wanted food; and to supply their hunger snatched a young little babe from the mothers breast, cutting off his arms and legs, cast a part of them to every dog, which they having devoured, he threw the remainder of the body to them. Thus it is plainly manifest how they value these poor creatures, created after the image of God, to cast them to their cannibal curs. But that which follows is (if possible) a sin of a deeper die.

I preterit their unparalleled impieties and only close all with this one Story that follows: Those haughty obdurate and execrable tyrants, who departed from this country to fish for riches in Persia and four Monks of the Order of St. Francis, with Father James who traveled there also to keep the country in peace and attract or mildly persuade by their reaching the remnant of inhabitants, that had outlived a septennial Tyranny, to embrace the knowledge of Christ. I conceive these are the persons who in the year 1534, traveling by Mexico were solicited by several messengers from the Indians, to come into their country and inform them in the knowledge of one God, the true God and Lord of the whole world. To this end they appointed assemblies and councils to examine and understand what men they were, who called themselves fathers and frier's, what they intended and what difference there was between them and the Spaniards, by whom they had been so molested and tormented, but they received them at length upon this condition that they should be admitted alone, without any Spaniards, which the Fathers promised for they had permission, an express mandate from the President of New Spain to make that promise, that the Spaniards should not do them the least harm. Then they began to preach the Gospel of Christ and to explicate and declare the pious intention of the King of Castile, of all which they had notice by the Spaniards for seven years together, that they had no King nor no other but him, who oppressed them with so much Tyranny. The Priests were there only forty days and they brought their Idols to be burned. Then they brought their children, which they tendered as the apple of the eye, that they might be instructed. They also erected temples and houses for them and they were desired to come to other Provinces and preach the Gospel and introduce them into the knowledge of God, and the Great (as they stiled him) King of Castile. The Priests persuasions wrought so effectually on them, that they condescended to that which was never done in India before (for whatsoever those Tyrants who wasted and consumed these large Kingdoms and Provinces, did misrepresent and falsify, was only done to bring an odium and disgrace upon the Indians). For twelve or fifteen princes of spacious and well-peopled Regions assembled, every one distinct and separate from the rest, with his own subjects and by their unanimous consent upon council and advice, of their own accord summited themselves to the government of the Castile's Kings and accepted them as their Prince and Protector, obliging themselves to obey and serve them as subjects to their lawful liege Lord.

In witness, where I have in my custody a certain instrument signed and attested by the said religiosity's.

Thus to the great joy and hope of these Priests, converting them to Christianity, they were received by the inhabitants of this Kingdom that survived the heat and rage of the Spanish cruelties. But behold, eighteen horsemen and twelve footmen, by another way crept in among them, bringing with them many Idols, which were of great weight and taken out of other Regions by force. The Commander in chief of these Spaniards summoned one of the rulers of that Province which they entered, to appear before him and command him to take these Idols with him, distribute them through his country and exchange every single Idol for an Indian man or woman, otherwise he would make war against him. The said Lord, compelled to it by fear, did so accordingly with a command that his subjects should adore worship and honor them and in compensation send Indian male and female into servitude. The terrified people delivered up their children, and by this means there was an end made of this sacrilegious merchandise and thus the Casic satisfied the greedy desires of the (I dare not say Christian) Spaniards. One of these sacrilegious robbers was John Garcia by name, who being very sick and at the point of death, had several Idols hidden under his bed, and calling his Indians that waited on him as a nurse, commanded her not to part with those Idols at a small rate, for they were of the better sort, that she should not dispose of them for any one Indian for each Idol by way of barter. By this, his private and non captive last Will and Testament, distracted with these carking cares, he gave up the Ghost. And who is it that will not fear his being tormented in the darkest and lowest Hell? Let us now consider what progress in Religion the Spaniards made, and what examples of Christianism they gave at their first arrival in America, how devoutly they honored God and what expense of sweat and toil they were at to promote his worship and adoration among the infidels. Let it be also taken into serious consideration, whose sin is the greater, either Jeroboam's, who made all Israel sin and caused two Golden Calves to be erected, or the Spaniards who traffic and trade in Idols like Judas, who was the occasion of such great scandals. These are the good deeds of the Spanish Dons, who very often, to feed their avarice and accumulate gold, have sold and still do sell, denied and still do deny, Jesus Christ our redeemer.

The Indians now finding the Promises of the Religious, that the Spaniards should not enter into this country, null and void; that the Spaniards brought Idols from other places to be dropped there when as they had delivered up their own to the Priests to be burnt, that there might be only worship of the true God established among them; they were highly incensed against these Friars and addressed themselves to them in these following words: "Why have you deceived us, binding your promises with false protestations, that the Spaniards should not be admitted to come hither? And why have you burnt our Gods, when others are brought from other Regions by the Spaniards? Are the Gods of other Provinces more sacred than ours?" The Friars, as well as they could (though they had little to return in answer), endeavored by soft language to appease them; and went to these thirty Spaniards, declaring the evil actions they were guilty of, humbly supplicating them to withdraw themselves from that place. Which they would by no means condescend to, and what is most flagitious and wicked persuaded the Indians, that they were introduced by those Priests, which being made known to them, these Indians resolved to be the death of these Monks. Having notice thereof by some courteous Indians, they stole away from there by night and fled. But after their departure, the truth of the matter and the Spanish malice being understood, they sent several messengers who followed them fifty miles distant beseeching them in the name of the Indians, to return and begging pardon for that ignorant mistake.

The Priests, relying on their words, returned and were caressed like angels sent from Heaven and continued with them, (from whom they received a thousand kindnesses) four or five months. But when the Spaniards persisted in their resolution not to quit the place, although they viceroy did use all endeavors and fair means to recall them, they were proclaimed traitors, guilty of high treason and because they continued still, exercising tyranny and perpetrated nefarious crimes, the Priests were sensible they would study revenge, though it might be some considerable time before they put it in execution, fearing that it might fail upon their own heads, and since they could not exercise the function of their Ministry securely and undisturbed by reason of the continual incursions and assaults made by the Spaniards, they discussed their departure and did leave this Kingdom accordingly which remained destitute of all Christian Doctrine. And these poor souls are at this day involved in the obscurity of their former misery and ignorance, they being deprived by these accursed Spaniards, of all hopes of remedy and the irrigation of Divine knowledge, just like young withering plants for want of water: for in that very juncture of time, when these religiosity's took leave, they embraced the Doctrine of our faith with the greatest fervency and eagerness imaginable.

Of the Province of St. Martha

The Province of St. Martha was rich in Golden Mines and a fruitful soil, the People were experts and industrious in those Mine-works. Upon this account or temptation it was, that from the year 1540 to 1542, an abundance of tyrants sailed there, laying waste the whole country by their depredations, slaughtering the inhabitants at a prodigious and bloody rate and robbing them of all their gold, who daily fled to their ships for refuge, moving sometime to one place and sometime to another. This is how those provinces laid to waste, the greatest outrages being committed on the seashore, which lasted till the year 1523, where the Spaniards then came to seat themselves and is their intended habitation. And because it is a plentiful Region and opulent with all, it was subjected to several Rulers, who like infernal fiends contended who should obtain the palm by out-staining the sword of his predecessor in innocent blood; insomuch, that from the year 1529 to this very day, they have wasted and spoiled as much good ground as extended five hundred miles and unpopulated the country.

If I designed to enumerate all the impieties, butcheries, desolations, iniquities, violences, destructions and other, the particular and black enormities committed and perpetrated by the Spaniards in this Province against God, the King and these harmless Nations; I might compile a voluminous history, and that shall be completed, if God permit my Glass to run longer, in his good time. It may suffice for the present to relate some passages written in a letter to our King and Lord by a Reverend Bishop of these Provinces, dated the 20th of May, An. Dom. 1541 where among other matters he said these words:

"I must acquaint your Sacred Majesty, that the only way to succor and support this tottering Region is to free it from the Power of a Father in Law, and marry it to a Husband who will treat her as she ought to be and lovingly entertain her, and that must be done with all possible expedition too. If not, I am certain that she will suddenly decay and come to nothing by the covetous and sordid deportment of the Governors". And a little after he writes "By this means, your Majesty will plainly know and understand how to depose the prefects or Governors of those Regions from their office if they deserve it, that so they may be alleviated and eased of such burthens; which if not performed, in my Opinion, the politic body will never recover its health. And this I will make appear to your Majesty, that they are not Christians, but Devils; not servants of God and the King, but traitors to the King and Laws, who are conversant in those Regions. And in reality nothing can be more obstructive to those that live peaceably, then inhumane and barbarous usage, which they who lead a quiet and peaceable life, too frequently undergo and this is so fastidious and nauseous to them, that there can be nothing in the world so odious and detestable among them as the name of a Christian: for they term the Christians in their Language *Yares*, that is, Devils; and in truth are not without reason; for the actions of those that reside in these Regions, are not such as speak them to be Christians or men gifted with reason, but absolute devils; hence it is, that the Indians, perceiving these actions committed by the heads as well as members, who are void of all compassion and humanity, do judge the Christian Laws to be of the same strain and temper and that their God and King are the authors of such enormities. Now to endeavor to work upon them a contrary persuasion is to no purpose; for this would afford them a greater latitude and liberty to deride Jesus Christ and his Laws. Now the Indians who protect and defend themselves by force of arms, think it more eligible and far better to die once than suffer several and many deaths under the Spanish power.

This I know experimentally, most Invincible Casar," And he adds farther, "Your Majesty is more powerful in subjects and servants, who frequent these Kingdoms, than you can imagine. Nor is there one Soldier among them all, who does not publicly and openly profess if he robs, steals, spoils, kills, burns his majesties subjects, 'tis to purchase gold: He will not say that he therein does your Majesty great Service, for they affirm they do it to obtain their own share and dividend. Wherefore, most Invincible Casar, it would be a very prudential act for your Majesty to testify by a rigid correction and severe punishment of some malefactors, that it is disservice to you for your subjects to commit such evil acts, as tend to the disobedience and dishonor of the Almighty".

What you have read here is in relation of the said Bishop of St. Martha, epitomized and extracted from his Letters, whereby it is manifest, how savagely they handle these mild and affable people. They term them warlike Indians, who take themselves to the mountains to secure themselves from Spanish cruelty and call them country Indians, or inhabitants, who by a dreadful massacre are delivered up to tyrannical and horrible servitude, whereby at length they are depopulated, made desolate and utterly destroyed; as appears by the epistle of the aforementioned Bishop, who only gives us a slight account or essay of their persecution and sufferings. The Indians of this country use to break out into such words as these, when they are driven, loaded like brutes through the uncouth ways in their journeys over the mountains, if they happen to faint through weakness and miscarry through extremity of Labor, (for then they are kicked and hit, their teeth dashed out with the pummels of their swords to raise them up again, when tired and fallen under weighty burthens and force them to go on without respiration or time to take breath and all this with the following inscription or upbraiding and taunting words: "O what a wicket Villain art thou?" (I say they burst out into these expressions) "I am absolutely tired, kill me, I desire to die, being weary of my life as well as my burthen and journey". And this with deep heartbreaking sighs, they being scarce able to draw or breathe out their words, which are the characteristic notes and infallible of the mind drowned in anguish and sorrow. My it please our Merciful God to order the discovery of these crimes to be manifested to those people who are able and obliged to redress them.

Of the Province of Cartagena

This Province fifty miles away from the Isle of St. Martha westward, and situated on the confines of the Country of Cenusia, from where it extends a hundred miles to the bay of Uraba and contains a very long tract of land southward. These Provinces from the year 1498 to this present time were most barbarously used and made desert by murder and slaughter, but that I may the sooner conclude this brief summary. I will not handle the particulars, to the end I may the better give an account of the detestable villainies that ruined other Regions.

Of the Pearl-Coast, Paria and Trinity-Isle

The Spaniards made great spoils and havoc from the Parian coast to the bay of Venezuela, exclusively, which is about two hundred miles.

It can hardly be expressed by tongue or pen how many and how great, injuries and injustices the inhabitants of this seashore have endured from the year 1510 to this day. I will only relate two or three piacular and criminal acts of the first magnitude, capable of comprehending all other enormities that deserve the sharpest torments, wit and malice can invent and so make way for a deserved judgment upon them.

A nameless pirate in the year 1510, accompanied with a parcel of sixty or seventy, arrived at Trinity-Island, which exceeds Sicily, both in amplitude and fertility, and is contiguous to the continent on that side where it touches upon Paria, whose inhabitants, according to their quality, are more addicted to probity and Virtue, than the rest of the Indians; who immediately published an edict, that all the inhabitants should come and cohabit with them. The Indian Lords and subjects gave them a debonair and brotherly Reception, serving them with wonderful alacrity, furnishing them with daily provisions in so plentiful a manner, that they might have sufficed a more numerous company; for it is the mode among Indians of this New World, to supply the Spaniards very bountifully with all manner of necessities.

A short time after the Spaniards built a stately house, which was an apartment for the Indians, that they might accomplish their premeditated designs, which was thus effected. When they were to thatch it, and had raised it two mens height, they enclosed several of them there, to expedite the work as they pretended, but in truth that they who were within, might not see those without; thus part of them surrounded the house with sword in hand that no one should stir out and part of them entered and bound the Indians, menacing them with death if they offered to move a foot;

and if any one endeavor to escape, he was presently hacked in pieces; but some of them partly wounded, and partly unwounded getting away, with others who went not into the house, about one hundred and two hundred, betook themselves to another house with bows and arrows. When they were all there, the Spaniards secured the doors, throwing in fire at another place, and so they all perished. From hence they set sail to the Island of St. John with near upon one hundred and eighty slaves, whom they had bound, where they sold one half of them and then to Hispaniola, where they disposed of the rest. Now when I taxed this Captain with wickedness and treachery in the very Isle of St. John, he dismissed me with this answer; "Forbear good Sir. I had this in commission from those who sent me here, that I should surprise them by the specious pretense of peace, whom I could not seize by open force" and in truth, this same Captain told me with his own mouth, that in Trinity-Isle alone, he had met with a father and mother in civil usage, which he uttered to his greater confusion and the aggravation of his sins. The Monks of our Order of St. Dominic on a certain time, held a consult about sending one of their fraternity into this Island, that by their reaching they might instruct them in the Christian faith and teach them the way to be saved, of which they were wholly ignorant. And to this end they sent there a religious and licentiate in Theology (or Doctor in Divinity, as we term it among us) a man famous for his virtue and Holiness with a Laic his associate, to visit the Country, converse with the Inhabitants and find out the most convenient places to build Monasteries. As soon as they arrived according to custom, they were entertained like celestial messengers, with great affection, joy and respect, as well as they could, for they were ignorant of their language and so made use of signs, for the present. It happened that after the departure of the vessel that brought these religious men, another came into the port, whose crew according to their hellish custom, fraudulently and unknown to the religious, brought away a Prince of that

Province as captive, who was called Alphonsus, (for they are ambitious of a Christian Name,) and with desire no more information, that he would baptize him. But the said Lord Alphonsus was deceitfully over persuaded to go on board of them with his wife and about seventeen more, pretending that they would give him a collation; which the Prince and they did, for he was confident that the religious would by no means abuse him, for he had no such confidence in the Spaniards; but as soon as they were upon deck, the perfidious rogues, set sail for Hispaniola, where they were sold as slaves. The whole country being extremely discomposed and understanding that their Prince and Princess were violently carried away, addressed themselves to these Religiosity's, who were in great danger of losing their Lives. But they, being made to understand this unjust action, were extraordinarily afflicted, and probably would have suffered death rather than permit the Indians to be so injuriously dealt with, which might prove an obstruction to their receiving of, and believing in God's Word. Yet the Indians were sedated by the promises of the religion; for they told them, they would send letters by the first ship that was bound for Hispaniola, whereby they would procure the restitution and return of their Lord and his retinue. It pleased God to send a ship there forthwith, to the greater confirming of the Governors damnation, where in the letters they sent to the religious of Hispaniola, letters containing repeated exclamations and protestations and protest against such actions, but those that received them denied them justice, for that they were partakers of that prey made of those Indians so unjustly and impiously captivated. But when the religious, who had engaged to the inhabitants, that their Lord Alphonsus should be restored within four months and found that neither in four nor eight months he was returned, they prepared to die and deliver their life to Christ, to whom they had offered it before their departure from Spain. Thus the innocent Indians were revenged on the innocent Priests; for they were of opinion, that the

64

religious had a hand in the plot, partly because they found their promises that their Lord should return within four months ineffectual, and partly because the inhabitants made no difference between a religious Friar and a Spanish rogue. At another time it fell out likewise, through the rampant tyranny and cruel deeds of evil-minded Christians, that the Indians put to death two Dominican Friars, of which I am a faithful witness, escaping my self not without a very great miracle, which transaction I resolve silently to pass over, lest I should terrify the reader with the horror of the fact.

In these Provinces, there was a City seated on the Bay of Codera, whose Lord was called Higueroto, a name, either proper to Persons or common to the Rulers of that place. A Cacic of such signal clemency, and his subjects of such noted virtue, that the Spaniards who went there were extraordinarily welcomed, furnished with provisions, enjoying peace and comfort and no refreshment wanting: But a perfidious wretch got many of them on board and sold them to the Islanders of St. John. At the same time I landed upon that Island, where I obtained a sight of this Tyrant, and heard the relation of his actions. He utterly destroyed that Land, which the rest of the Spaniards took very unkindly at his hands, who frequently played the pirate, and robbed on that shore, detesting it as a wicked thing, because they had lost that place, where they use to be treated with as great hospitality and freedom, as if they had been under their own roof. No, they transported from this place, among them, to the Isles of Hispaniola and St. John over two million men and made the coast a desert.

It is most certainly true, that they never ship off a vessel freighted with Indians, but they pay a third part as tribute to the Sea, besides those who are slaughtered, when found in their own homes. Now the source and original of all this is the ends they have proposed to themselves. For there is a necessity of taking with them a great number of Indians, that they may gain a great sum of money by their sale, now the ships are very slenderly furnished with provisions and water in small quantity, to satisfy few, left the Tyrants, who are termed owners or proprietors of ships should be at too great expense in victualing their vessels, they hardly carry food enough with them to maintain the Spaniards that manage the vessel, which is the reason so many Indians die of hunger and thirst and of necessity they must be thrown over-board. One of them told me this for a truth, that there being such a multitude of men thus destroyed, a Ship may sail from the Isle of Lucaya to Hispaniola, which is a voyage of over twenty leagues without chart or compass, by the sole direction or observation of dead fluctuating Carcasses.

But afterward, when arrived and driven up into the Isle where they are brought to be sold, there is no Person that is in some small measure compassionate, but would be extremely moved and discomposed at the sight; to spy on old men and women, together with naked children half starved. Then they separate parents from children, wives from their husbands, about Ten or Twenty in a company and cast lots for them, that the detestable owners of the ships may have their share; who prepare two or three ships and equip them as a fleet of pirates, going ashore ravaging and forcing men out of their homes and then robbing them. But when the lot of any one of them falls upon a parcel that has an aged or diseased man, the Tyrant, whose allotment he is, usually bursts out, as follows: "Let this old fellow be Dammed, why do you bestow him upon me; must I, think you; be at the charge of his Burial? And this sickly wretch, how comes he to be one of my alloted portion must I take care for his cure? Not I." Hence you may guess what estimate and value the Spaniards put upon Indians, and whether they practice and fulfill that Divine and Heavenly precept enjoying mutual love and society.

There can be nothing more cruel and detestable then the

Tyrannical usage of the Spaniards towards the Indians in their pearl-fishing; for the torments undergone in the unnatural exenteration and tearing out with parricidal hands the richer bowels of our common mother or the inward excruciating racks of the most profligate, Heaven daring desperado can admit of no comparison with these, although the extracting or digging for gold is one of the sharpest subterranean drudgeries, they plunge them down four or five ells deep under water, where swimming about without breathing, they eradicate and pull up oysters, where the pearls are engendered. Sometimes they rise up to the superficies of the water with nets full of oysters for respiration and air, but if these miserable creatures stay but a little more than is ordinary to rest themselves, the hangman is immediately upon them in a canoe or small boat, who beating them with many stripes drag them by the hair of the head under water, that they may drudge again at their explication or pearl fishing. Their food is fish and the same which contains the pearls and cassabus made of roots with a few mahids, the bread of that country; in the former there is little or no nutriment or substance, and the other is not made without great trouble, nor for all this have they a sufficient allowance thereof to support nature. Their lodging or bed is the earth confined to a pair of stocks, for fear that they should run away: And it frequently happens that they are drowned with the toil of this kind of fishing and never more seen, for the Tuberoms and Maroxi (certain Marine Monsters that devour a complete proportioned man wholly at once) prey upon them under water. You must consider with all, that it is impossible for the strongest constitution to continue long under water without breathing and they ordinarily die through the extream rigor of the cold, spitting blood which is occasioned by the too great compression of the breast, procreated by a continued holding breath under water, for by too much cold a profluvium of blood follows. Their hair naturally black is changed into a combustive, burnt or Sun-color like that of the sea wolves, their shoulders and backs covered, or overspread with a saltish humor that they appear rather like monsters in humane shape then men.

They have destroyed all the Lucayans by this intolerable or rather diabolical exercise, for the accustomed emolument or gain of lucre, and by this means gained the value of fifty, sometimes one hundred crowns of every individual Indian. They sell them (though it is prohibited) publicly; for the Lucayans were excellent swimmers and several perished in this Isle that came from other Provinces.

Of the River Yuya Pari

This River washes the Province arising from its head or fountain in another Region, two hundred miles off and better. By this, a wretched Tyrant entered it and laid waste the Land for the space of many miles and murdered abundance of them by fire and sword. At length he died violently, and all his forces moldered away of themselves, many succeeded him in his iniquity and cruelty and so daily destroy them, sending to Hell the souls redeemed by the blood of the Son of God.

Of the Kingdom of Venezuela

Our Sovereign Lord the King in the year 1526, persuaded by fallacious appearances (for the Spaniards use to conceal from His Majesties knowledge the damages and detriments, which God himself, the souls and state of the Indians did suffer) entrusted the Kingdom of Venezuela longer and larger then the Spanish dominions, with its Government and absolute jurisdiction to some German merchants, with power to make certain capitulations and conventions, who came into this Kingdom with three hundred men and there found a benign mild and peaceable people, as they were throughout the Indies till injured by the Spaniards. These more cruel than the rest beyond comparison, behaved themselves more inhumanely then rapacious tigers, wolves and lions, for they had the jurisdiction in this Kingdom and therefore possessing it with the greater freedom from control, lay in wait and were the more vigilant with greater care and avarice to understand the practical part of heaping up wealth and robbing the inhabitants of their gold and sliver, surpassing all their predecessors in those indirect ways, rejecting wholly both the fear of their God and King, forgetting that they were born men with reasonable faculties.

These incarnate devils laid waste and desolate four hundred miles of most fertile land, containing vast and wonderful provinces, most spacious and large valleys surrounded with hills, forty miles in length, and many towns richly abounding in gold and silver. They destroyed so many and such considerable regions, that there is not one spare witness left to relate the story, unless perchance some that lurked in the caverns and womb of the earth to evade death by their inhumane swords filled with innocent Indian blood, escaped. I judge that they, by new invented and unusual torments, ruined four or five million of souls and sent them all to Hell. I will give a taste of two or three of their transactions, so that you may guess at the rest.

They made the supreme Lord of the Province a slave, to squeeze his gold from him, torturing him to confess who fled into the mountains, their common sanctuary, and his subjects lying absconded in the thickets of the woods, were stirred into sedition and tumult or mutiny. The Spaniards follow and destroy many of them, but those that were taken alive and in their power were all publicly sold for slaves by the common crier.

They were, in all the Provinces they entered, entertained and welcomed by the Indians with songs, dances and rich presents but rewarded very ungratefully with bloodshed and slaughter. The German Captain and Tyrant caused several of them to be chained to a Thatcht House, and there cut in pieces; but some of them to avoid falling by their bloody and merciless swords, climbed up to the beams and rafters of the house and the governor, hearing it (O cruel Brute?) commanded them to burn it with them all alive leaving the Region desert and desolate.

They also came to another stately Province, bordering on St. Martha, whose inhabitants did them many egregious and notable services, bestowing them with quantities of gold besides many other gifts, but when they were upon departure, in retribution of their civil treating and deportment the German Tyrant, commanded that all the Indians, with their wives and children if possible, should be taken into custody; enclosed in some large capacious place, only to be set at liberty those who should redeem themselves at the will and pleasure (as to price) of the unjust governor, or at a certain rate imposed on them, their wives and every child's head, and to expedite the prohibition of the administration or allowance of any food to them till the gold required for redemption was paid down to the utmost grain. Several of them sent home to discharge the demanded price of their redemption and procured their freedom as well as they could by one means or other, that so they might return to their livelihood and profession, but not long after he sent other rogues and robbers among them to enslave those that were redeemed.

To the same Gaol they are brought a second time, being instigated or rather constrained to a speedy redemption by hunger and thirst; Thus many were taken, two or three times, captive and then redeemed some who were not capable of depositing such a sum, perished there. Furthermore, this Tyrant was big with an itching desire after the discovery of the Peruvian Mines, which he accomplished. I should not number the particular cruelties and slaughters committed by him though my discourse would not in the least be contrary to the truth, yet it would not be believed and only stupefy and amaze the reader.

This course the other Tyrants took, who set sail from Venezuela and St. Martha (with the same resolution of detecting the Peruvian Golden, consecrated houses as them they esteemed) who found the fruitful Region so desolate, deserted and wasted by fire and sword, that those cruel Tyrants themselves were smitten with wonder and astonishment at the traces and ruins of such prodigious devastations.

All these things and many more were proved by witness in the Indian exchequer and the records of their testimony were entered in that court, though these execrable Tyrants burnt so many that there might be little or nothing proved of those great devastations and evils perpetrated by them. For the minister of justice who have then lived in India, through their obscure and damnable blindness, were not much solicitous about the punishment of the crimes and butcheries which have been and are still committed by these Tyrants. Only they may say, possibly because so and so has wickedly and barbarously dealt with the Indians, that is the reason so great a sum of Crowns in money is diminished already or retrenched from His Majesties annual revenue, and this general and confused proof is sufficient (as they worthily conceive) to purge or repress such great and heinous crimes. And though they are but few, are not verified as they ought to be, nor do they attribute and lay upon them that stress and weight as they ought to do, for if they did perform their duty to God and the King, it could not be made apparent as it may be, that these German Tyrants have cheated and robbed the King of over three million in gold. These enemies to God and King began to depopulate these regions and destroy them, cheating his Majesty of two million in gold per annum, nor can it be expected, that the detriment done to his Majesty can possibly be retrieved, as long as the sun and moon endures, unless God by a miracle should raise as many thousands from death to life, as were destroyed. And these are the temporal damages the King suffers. It would also be a work worthy inquiry, to consider how many cursed sacrileges and indignities God himself has been affronted with to the dishonor of his Name. And what recompense can be made for the loss of so many souls as are now tormented in Hell by the cruelty and covetousness of these brutish German Tyrants. But I will conclude, all their impiety and barbarism with one example: That from the time they entered this Country to this very day, seventeen years in all, they have remitted many ships freighted with Indians to be sold as slaves to the Isles of St. Martha, Hispaniola, Jamaica and St. John, selling a million people at the least, I speak modestly, and still do expose to sale to this very year of our Lord 1542, the King's Council in this Island seeing and knowing it. Yet what they find to be manifest and apparent, they connive at, permit and countenance and wink at the horrid impieties and innumerable devastations which are committed on the coasts of this continent, extending four hundred miles in length and continues still together with Venezuela and St. Martha under their jurisdiction, which they might easily have remedied and timely prevented.

Of the Provinces of Florida

Three Tyrants at several times made their entrance into these Provinces since the year 1510 or 1511, to act those crimes which others, and two of these Three made it their sole business to do in other Regions, to the end, that they might advance themselves to higher dignities and promotions than they could deserve, by the effusion of blood and destruction of these people. But at length they all were cut off by a violent death, and the homes which they formerly built with the cement of human blood, (which I can sufficiently testify of these three) perished with them, and their memory rotten, and as absolutely washed away from off the face of the earth, as if they had never been. These men deserted these Regions, leaving them in great distraction and confusion, nor were they branded with less notes of infamy, by the certain slaughters they perpetrated, though they were but few in number than the rest. For the Just God cut them off before they did much mischief, and reserved the castigation and revenge of those evils which I know and was an eye-witness of, to this very time and place. As to the fourth Tyrant, who lately, that is in the year 1538, went there well-furnished with men and ammunition, we have received no account of in the past three years, but are very confident, that he, at his first arrival, acted like a bloody Tyrant, even to ecstasy and madness, if he is still alive with his follower, and did injure, destroy, and consume a vast number of men (for he was branded with infamous cruelty above all those who with their assistants committed crimes and enormities of the first magnitude in these Kingdoms and Provinces) I conceive, God has punished him with the same violent death, as he did other Tyrants. But because my pen is wearied with relating such execrable and sanguinary deeds (not of men but beasts) I will trouble my self no longer with the dismal and fatal consequences thereof.

They found these people to be wise, grave and well disposed, though their usual butcheries and cruelties in oppressing them like brutes, with heavy burthens, did rack their minds with great terror and anguish. At their entry into a certain village, they were welcomed with great joy and exultation, replenished them with victuals, till they were all satisfied, giving them over six hundred men to carry their bags and baggage, and grooms to look after their horses. The Spaniards departing then, a Captain related to the Superior Tyrant, returned there to rob these (no ways diffident or mistrustful) People, and pierced their King through with a lance, of which wound he died upon the spot, and committed several other cruelties into the bargain. In another neighboring town, whose inhabitants they thought were more vigilant and watchful, having had the news of their horrid acts and deeds, they barbarously murdered them all with their lances and swords, destroying all, young and old, great and small, lords and subject without exception.

The Chief Tyrant caused many Indians (over two hundred as heard abroad) whom he summoned to appear before him out of another town, or else, who came voluntarily to pay their respects to him, to have their noses and lips to the very beard cut off, and in this grievous and wretched condition, the blood gushing out of their wounds, returned them back to give an infallible testimony of the works and miracles wrought by these Preachers and Ministers baptized in the Catholic faith.

Now let all men judge what affection and love they bear to Christianity; to what purpose or upon what account they believe there is a God, whom they preach and boast of to be Good and Just, and that his Law which they profess (and indeed only profess) to be pure and immaculate. The mischiefs acted by these profligate wretches and sons of perdition were of the deepest die. At last this Captain devoted to perdition died impenitent, nor do we in the least question, but that he is overwhelmed and buried in darkness infernal, unless God according to his infinite mercy and boundless clemency, not his own merits, (he being contaminated and poisoned with execrable deeds,) be pleased to compassionate and have mercy upon him.

Of the Plate-River, that is, the Silver-River

Some Captains since the year 1502 to 1503 undertook four or five voyages to the River of Plate, which embraces within its own arms great Kingdoms and Provinces, and is peopled by rational and well-tempered inhabitants. In the general we are certified, that they were very injurious and bloody to them; but they being far distant from those Indians, were not able to give you a particular account of their transactions. Yet beyond all controversy, they did and still do go the same way to work, as others in several Regions to this present time do, and have done. For they are the same (and many in number too) Spaniards who went there, that were the wicked instruments of other executions, and all of them aim at one and the same thing; namely to grow rich and wealthy, which they can never be, unless they steer the same course which others have followed, and tread the same paths in murdering, robbing and destroying poor Indians.

After I had committed to writing what I have premonition, it was told to me in truth, that they had laid waste in those Countries great Kingdoms and Provinces, dealing cruelly and bloody with these harmless People, at a horrid rate, having a greater opportunity and convenience to be more infamous and rigid to them, than others, they being very remote from Spain, living inordinately, like debauches, laying aside and bidding farewell to all manner of justice, which is indeed a stranger in all the American Regions, as we stated already. But among the other numerous wicked acts following this is one, that may be read in the Indians Courts. One of the Governors commanded his soldiers to go to a certain village, and if they denied them provisions, to put kill all the inhabitants. By virtue of this authority they marched and because they would not yield to them over five thousand men as enemies, fearing rather to be seen than guilty of illiberality, were murdered. Also a certain number of men living in peace and tranquility proffered their services to him; who, as it fell out, were called before the governor, but deferring their appearance a little longer than ordinary that he might infix their minds with a remark of horrible Tyranny, he commanded them to be delivered as prisoners to their mortal Indian enemies, who begged loudly with a deluge of tears, to kill themselves rather than be given up as a prey to the enemy; but in resolution, they would not the leave the house they were in, so the Spaniards hacked them to pieces limb by limb, who exclaimed and cried aloud, "We came to visit and serve you peaceably and quietly and you murder us; our blood with which these walls are moistened and sprinkled will remain as an everlasting testimony of our unjust slaughter and your barbarous cruelty. And really this horrid crime deserves a commemoration, or rather speak more properly, the commiseration of all persons."

Of the vast Kingdoms and Spacious Provinces of Perusia

A notorious Tyrant in the year 1531, entered Perusia with his soldiers, and with the same pretenses began at the same rate as others did; he indeed being one of those who were exercised and highly concerned in the slaughters and cruelties committed on the continent ever since the year 1510, he increased and heightened the cruelties, butcheries and rape; destroying and laying waste (being a false-hearted faithless person) the towns and villages, murdering the inhabitants, which occasioned all those evils that succeeded in those regions afterward. Now to undertake the writing of a narrative of them and represent them lively and naturally to the readers view and perusal, is a work altogether impossible but must lie concealed and unknown until they shall more openly and clearly appear and be made visible to every eye at the day of Judgment. As for my part, if I should presume to unravel, in some measure the deformity, quality and circumstances of those enormities, I must ingenuously confess I could by no means perform so burdensome a task, and render it complete and as it ought to be.

At his first admission into these parts, he had laid waste some towers and robbed them of a great quantity of gold. This he did in the infancy of his tyrannical attempts, when he arrived at Pugna, a neighboring Isle, he had the reception of an angel; but about six months later, when the Spaniards had spent all their provisions, they discovered and opened the Indians stores and granaries, which were made fort heir own sustenance, wives and children against a time of dearth and scarcity, brought them forth with tears and weepings, to dispose of at pleasure. But they rewarded them with slaughter, slavery and depopulation as formerly.

After that, they went to the Isle Tumbala, situated on the firm land where they killed all they met with. And because the people, terrified with their abominable sins of commission, fled from their cruelty, they were accused of rebellion against the Spanish King. This Tyrant made use of this artifice, he commanded all that he took or that had bestowed gold, silver and other rich gifts on him, still to load him with other presents, till he found they had exhausted their treasures, and were grown naked and incapable of affording him farther supplies. So he declared them to be the vassals and subjects of the King of Spain, flattering them and proclaiming twice by sound of trumpet, that for the future he would not captivate or molest them any more, looking upon it as lawful to rob and terrify them with such messages as he had done, before he admitted them under the King's protection, as if from that very time he had never robbed, destroyed or oppressed them with tyrannical usage.

Not long after Ataliba the King and Supreme Emperor of all these Kingdoms, leading a great number of naked men, he himself being at the head of them, armed with ridiculous weapons and wholly ignorant of the goodness of the Spaniards Bilbo-blades, the mortal darings of their lances, and the Strength of their horse, whose use and service was to him altogether unknown and never so much as heard of before, that the Spaniards were sufficiently armed to rob the devils themselves of gold, if they had any, came to the place where they were saying,"Where are these Spaniards? Let them appear, I will not stir a foot from hence till they give me satisfaction for my subjects whom they have slain, my towns they have reduced to ashes and my riches they have stolen from me". The Spaniards meet him, make a great slaughter of his men and seize on the King himself, who was carried in a chair on mens shoulders. There was a treaty for his redemption, the King agreed to lay down four million Crowns, as the purchase of his freedom, but fifteen were paid down upon the nail. They promise to set him at liberty, but contrary to all faith and truth according to their common custom (for they always violated their promises with the Indians) they falsely imposed this upon him, that his people united by his command, but the King was answered that throughout his dominions, not so much as a leaf upon a tree durst move without his authority and pleasure, and if any were assembled together, they must of necessity believe that it was done without his order, he being a captive, it being in their power to deprive him of his life, if any such thing should be ordered by him. Notwithstanding which, they consulted to have him burn alive, and a little while after the sentence was agreed upon, but the Captain by request of some people, commanded him first to be strangled and afterward thrown into the fire. The King, understanding the sentence of death past upon him, said; "Why do you burn me? What fact have I committed deserving death? Did you not promise to set me free for a sum of gold? And did I not give you a far larger quantity than I promised? But if it is your pleasure so to do, send me to your King of Spain" and by using many words to the same purpose, confusing and detesting the Spanish Injustice, he was burnt to death. And here let us take into serious consideration the right and title they had to make this war, the captivity, sentence and execution of this King and the conscience these Tyrants have possessed themselves of vast treasures, which they have surreptitiously and fraudulently taken away from this King, and a great many more of the rulers of these Kingdoms. But as to the great number of their enormities committed by those who stile themselves Christians, in order to the extirpation of this people, I will repeat some of them, which in the very beginning were seen by a Franciscan, confirmed by his own letters and signed with his hand and seal, sending some of them to the Peruvian Provinces and others to the Kingdom of Castile. A copy which I have in my custody, signed with his hand, as I said before and the contents are as follows:

"I Friar Marcus De Xlicia, of the Franciscan Order and Prefect of the whole Fraternity residing in the Peruvian Provinces, one of the first among the Religious, who arrived with the Spaniards in these parts. I declare with incontrovertible and undeniable testimony, those transactions which I saw with my own eyes, and particularly such as relate to the usage of the inhabitants of this Region. In the first place I was an eye-witness, and am certainly assured that these Peruvians are a people, who transcend all other Indians in meekness, clemency and love to Spaniards, and I have seen the Indians bestow very liberally on them gold, silver and jewels, being very serviceable to them in many other ways. Nor did the Indians ever betake themselves to their arms in a hostile manner, till by infinite injuries and cruelties they were compelled thereunto; For on the contrary, they gave the Spaniards an amicable and honorable reception in all their towns and supplied them with provisions and as many male and female servants as they required.

I can also farther testify, that the Spaniards without the least provocation on their part, as soon as they entered these Territories, did burn at the stake their most potent Casic Ataliba, Prince of the whole Country, after they had extorted from him above two millions of gold, and possessed themselves of his Province, without the least opposition, and Cochilimaca, his Captain General, who with other Rulers, came peaceably to them, followed him by the same fiery trial and death. As also some few days after, the Ruler of the Province of Quitonia, who was burnt without any cause given or crime laid to his charge. They likewise put Schapera, Prince of the Canaries to the same death, and in like manner burnt the feet of Alvidis, the greatest of all the Quitonian Lords, and racked him with other torments to extract from him a discovery of Ataliba's treasure, whereof as appeared after, he was totally ignorant. Thus they treated Cocopaganga, governor of all the Provinces of Quitonia, who being overcome with the entreaties of Sebastian Bernalcarus, the Governors Captain, went peaceably to pay them a visit; but because he could not give them as much gold as they demanded, they burnt him with many other Casics and chief persons of quality. And as I understand, did it with this evil intention, that they might not leave one surviving lord or peer in the whole country.

I also affirm that I saw with these eyes of mine the Spaniards for no other reason, but only to gratify their bloody mindedness, cut off the hands, noses and ears, both of Indians and Indianesses, and that in so many places and parts, that it would be too prolix and tedious to relate them. Nay, I have seen the Spaniards let loose their dogs upon the Indians to bait and tear them in pieces, and such a number of villages burnt by them as cannot well be discovered. Farther this is a certain Truth, that they snatched babes from the mothers embraces and taking hold of their arms threw them away as far as they would from them (a pretty kind of Barr-tossing recreation). They committed many other cruelties, which shook me with terror at the very sight of them, and would take up too much time in the relation.

I likewise aver, that the Spaniards gathered together as many Indians as filled three houses, to which for no cause (or a very inconsiderable one) they set fire, and burnt every one of them. But a Presbyter, Ocana by Name, chanced to snatch a little baby out of the fire, which being observed by a Spaniard, he tore him out of his arms and threw him into the midst of the flames, where he was with the rest soon burnt to ashes, which Spaniard the same day he committed that fact, returning to his quarters, died suddenly by the way and I advised them not to give him Christian burial.

Furthermore I saw them send to several Casics and Principal Indians, promising them a protecting passport to travel peaceably and securely to them, who no sooner came, but they were burnt; two of them before my face, one at Andonia and the other at Tumbala, nor could I with all my persuasions and reaching to them prevail so far as to save them from the fire. And this I do maintain according to God and my own conscience, as far as I could possibly learn, that the inhabitants of Perusia never promoted or raised any commotion or rebellion, though as it is manifest to all men, they were afflicted with evil dealings and cruel torments; and they, not without cause, the Spaniards breaking their faith and word, betraying the truth and tyrannically contrary to all law and justice, destroying them and the whole country, inflicting on them great injuries and losses, were more ready to prepare themselves for death, than still to fall at once into such great and irrecoverable miseries.

Nay I do declare, according to information from the Indians themselves, that there are to this day far greater Quantities of gold kept hid and concealed than ever were yet detected or brought to light, which by means of the Spanish injustice and cruelty, they would not then nor ever will, discover so long as they are so barbarously treated, but will rather chose to die with the herd. Whereat the Lord God is highly offended and the King has very ill offices done him, for he is hereby defrauded of this Region, which was sufficiently able to furnish all Castile with necessaries, the recovery whereof can never be expected without great difficulty and vast expenses.

Thus far I have acquainted you with the very words of this religious Franciscan, ratified by the Bishop of Mexico, who testifies that the said Friar Marc did affirm and maintain what is above-mentioned."

Here it is to be observed what this said Friar was an eye-witness of; for he traveled up in this country fifty or a hundred miles in nine or ten years, when as yet, few Spaniards have footing there, but after hearing of the quantities of gold to be had there, four or five thousand went there, who spread through those Kingdoms and Provinces a space of five or six hundred miles, which they desolated completely, committing the same and greater cruelties than are before recited. For in reality they killed from that time to these very days, over a hundred thousand poor souls more than he gives an account of, and with less fear of God and the King, even less mercy, they destroyed the greatest part of mankind in these Kingdoms, over four millions suffering by violent death.

A few days after they darted to death with arrows made of reeds, a Puissant Queen, the wife of a Potentate who still sways the Imperial scepter of that Kingdom, whom the Spaniards had a design to take, instigated him to raise a rebellion and he still continues a rebel. They seized the Queen his consort, and contrary to all law and equity murdered her, as said before, who was then, as report, big with child, only so that they might add fresh affliction and grief to her husband.

Of the New Kingdom of Granada

Many Tyrants there were, who set sail from Venezuela, St. Martha and Cartagena, hastening to the conquest of Perusia, Anno Dom. 1539 and they, accompanied with many more, going farther from this Region, endeavored to penetrate into the heart of this country, where they found about three hundred miles from Cartagena and St. Martha, many admirable Provinces and most fruitful lands furnished with an even-tempered or meek-spirited People, as they are in other parts of India. Very rich in gold and those sorts of precious stones known by the name of emeralds. To which Province they gave the name of Granada upon this account, because the Tyrant who first arrived in these Regions, was born in the Kingdom of Granada belonging to these parts. They that spoiled these Provinces with their raping, being wicked, cruel, infamous butchers and delighting in the effusion of humane blood, having practically experimented the piacular and grand enormities perpetrated among the Indians, and upon this account their diabolical actions are so great, so many in number, and represented so grievously horrid by circumstantial aggravations, that they exceed all the villainies committed by others and themselves in other Regions, I will only select and call out a few out of so great a number which have been transacted by them within these three years, for my present purpose.

A certain governor, because he that went to commit depredations and spoils in the Kingdom of Granada, would not admit him as a companion in his robberies and cruelties, set up an inquisition and produced proofs confirmed by great evidence, where he palpably lays open and proves the slaughters and homicides he committed, and persists in to this very day, which were read in the Indian Courts of judicature and are there now recorded.

In this inquisition, the witnesses depose that when all these Kingdoms enjoyed peace and tranquility, the Indians served the Spaniards and got their living by constant day-labor in tilling and manuring the ground, bringing them much gold and gems, particularly emeralds, and what other commodities they could and possessed their cities and dominions being divided among the Spaniards, to procure which is the chiefest of their care and pains, and these are the proper measures they take to obtain their proposed ends, to wit, heaping and treasuring up of gold and riches.

Now when all the Indians were under their accustomed tyranny, a certain Tyrant, and Chief Commander, took the King and Lord of the whole country and detained him captive for six or seven months, demanding of him without any reason,a store of gold and Emeralds. The said King, whose name was Bogoca, through fear, promised him a house of gold, hoping, in time, to escape out of his clutches, who plagued him and sent some Indians for gold, who frequently and at several times, brought him a great quantity of gold and many jewels, but because the King did not, according to his promise, bestow upon him an apartment made of pure gold, he must therefore forfeit his life.

The Tyrant commanded him to be brought to trial before him so they may cite and summon to a trial the greatest King in the whole Region, and the Tyrant pronounced this sentence, that unless he did perform his golden promise, he should be exposed to severe torments. They racked him, poured boiling soap into his bowels, chained his legs to one post and fastened his neck to another, two men holding his hands and so applied the scorching heat of the fire to his feet. The Tyrant himself often casting his eye upon him, and threating him with death if he did not give him the promised gold; and with these kind of horrid torments, the said lord was killed, which while they were doing, God being willing to manifest how displeasing these cruelties are to His Divine Majesty, the whole city where this was taking place, was consumed by fire; and the rest of the Captains, following his example, destroyed all the lords of that region by fire and faggot.

Once it happened, that many Indians addressed themselves to the Spaniards with all humility and simplicity as they used to do, who thinking themselves safe and secure, as the Captain comes into the city, where they were to do their work, and commands all these Indians, sleeping and taking their rest after supper, being wearied with the heavy drudgery of the day, to be slaughtered. And this strategy he put in practice, to make a greater impression of fear on all the minds of the inhabitants. Another time, a certain Captain commanded the Spaniards to declare upon oath, how many Casics and Indians every individual person had in his family at home, who were presently lead to a public place to be beheaded, there perishing about four or five hundred men. The witnesses depose this of a particular Tyrant, that by beating, cutting off the hands and noses of many women as well as men, and killing several persons in great numbers, he exercised horrid cruelties.

Then one of the Captains sent this bloody Tyrant into the Province of Bogata, to inquire who succeeded the Prince there, whom he so barbarously and inhumanely murdered, who traveling many miles in this country, took as many Indians as he could get, some of which, because they did not tell him who was successor of this deceased Prince, had their hands cut off and others were devoured by hunger, many perishing miserably.

Another time, early in the morning, he fell upon several Casics, noblemen and other Indians, who thought themselves to be safe enough, (for they had their faith and security given, that none of them should receive any damage or injury) relying upon this, they left the mountains, their lurking places, without any suspicion or fear, returning to their Cities, but he seized them all and commanded them to extend their hands on the ground, cut them off with his own sword, saying that he punished them after in this manner because they would not inform him what lord it was that succeeded in that Kingdom.

The inhabitants of one of these Provinces, perceiving that four or five of their Governors were sent to the other world in a fiery vehicle or chariot, being terrified, fled to the mountains for sanctuary, there being four or five thousand in number, as appears by good evidence. So the Captain sends a Tyrant, more cruel than any of the rest, after them. The Spaniards ascend the mountains by force (for the Indians were naked an unarmed) proclaiming peace if they would desist and lay down their arms, which the Indians no sooner heard but lowered their childish weapons, and this was no sooner done but this sanguinary Spaniard sent some to possess themselves of the fortifications and they being secured, attacked the Indians. Thus they, like wolves and lions, rushed upon this flock of sheep and were so tired with slaughter, that they were forced to desist for a while and take breath, which done, the Captain commands them to fall to it again at the same bloody rate and hurry all that survived the butchery from the top of the mountain, which was of a prodigious height; and that was performed accordingly. The witnesses farther declare upon oath, that they saw the bodies of about seven hundred Indians falling from the mountain at one time, like a cloud obscuring the air, who were all broken to pieces.

This very Tyrant came once to the city Cota, where he surprised an abundance of men, together with fifteen or twenty Casics of the highest rank and quality, whom he cast to the dogs to be torn limb-meal in pieces and cut off the hands of several men and women, which being run through with a pole, were exposed to be viewed and gazed upon by the Indians, where you might see at once seventy pairs of hands, transfixed with poles; nor is it to be forgotten, that he cut off the noses of many women and children.

The Witnesses farther depose, that the cruelties and great slaughters committed in the new Kingdom of Granada by this Captain, and other Tyrants, the destroyers of mankind, who accompany him and still have the power to exercise the same, are so heinous, that if his Majesty does not opportunely fix, redress and prevent such mischiefs in the future (since the Indians, being robbed by the Spaniards of their gold, are being slaughtered and have no gold left to give), the Kingdom will decay and be made desolate, consequently being a land destitute of Indians, will lie uncultivated.

And here is to be noted, how pestilential and inhumane the cruelty of these Tyrants has been, and how violently exercised, when as in two or three years they were all slain, and the country wholly desolate and deserted, as those that have been eye-witnesses can testify. They having acted like merciless men, not having the fear of God and the King before their eyes, but by the instigation of the devil, so that it may well be said and affirmed, not one person will be left alive, unless his Majesty does retard and put a stop to the full career of their cruelties, which I am very apt to believe, for I have seen with these very eyes of mine, many Kingdoms laid waste and depopulated in a small time. There are other stately Provinces on the confines of the New Kingdom of Granada, as Popayan and Cali, that are together over five hundred miles in length, which they destroyed in the same manner as they have done other places, and laid them absolutely waste by the mentioned slaughters, who were populated and the soil very fruitful. They who came among us from those Regions report, that nothing can be more deplorable or worthy of pity and commiseration, than to behold such large and great Cities totally ruined and entombed in their own ashes, and that in a city adorned with 1000 or 2000 fabrics, there are hardly now to be seen 50 standing, the rest being utterly demolished or consumed and leveled to the ground by fire and in some parts Regions of 100 miles in length, (containing spacious Cities) are found absolutely destroyed and consumed by fire.

Finally many great Tyrants who came out of the Peruvian Kingdoms by the Quitonians, traveled to the new Kingdom of Granada and Popayan, and by Cartagena and the Urabae they directed their course to Calisium and several other Tyrants of Cartagena assault Quito, who united with them, depopulated and laid waste whole regions in of over 600 mile radius, with the loss of a prodigious number of poor souls. Nor as yet do they treat the small remnant of so great and innocent a people with more humanity than formerly.

I desire therefore that the readers who have or shall peruse these passages, would please seriously consider whether or not such barbarous, cruel and inhumane acts as these do not transcend and exceed all the impiety and tyranny which can enter into the thoughts or imagination of man, and whether these Spaniards deserve not the name of devils. For which of these two things is more eligible or desirable whether the Indians should be delivered up to the devils themselves to be tormented or the Spaniards? That is still a question.

I cannot omit hear one piece of villainy (whether it ought to be postponed or come behind the cruelty of brute animals, that I leave to decision). The Spaniards who are conversant among the Indians, bred such birds that are so well instructed and taught that they at first sight, fly upon the inhabitants tearing them limb by limb, devouring them. Now let all people, whether Christians or not consider, if ever such a thing as this reached the ears of any man, they carry these dogs with them as companions where ever they go and kill the fettered Indians in multitudes like hogs for their food and sharing with them in the butchery. They frequently call one to the other, saying "lend me the fourth part of one of your slaves to feed my dogs, and when I kill one I will repay you" as if they had only borrowed a quarter of a hog or sheep. Others, when they go a hunting early in the morning, upon their return, if you ask them what sport had you to day at the game? They will answer,"enough, enough, for my dogs have killed and worried 15 or 20 Indian vassals". Now all these things plainly prove those inquisitions and examinations made by one Tyrant against another. What, I beseech you, can be more horrid or barbarous?

But I will desist from writing any longer at this time, till some messenger brings an account of greater and blacker impieties (if greater can be committed) or else till we come to behold them again, as we have done in forty two years with our own eyes. I will only make this small addition to what I have said: that the Spaniards, from the beginning of their first entrance upon America to this present day, were no more solicitous of promoting the reaching of the Gospel of Christ to these nations, than if they had been dogs or beasts, but which is worst of all, they expressly prohibited their addresses to the religious, laying many heavy impositions upon them, daily afflicting and persecuting them, that they might not have so much time and leisure at their own disposal, as to attend their preaching and divine service; for they saw upon that to be an impediment to their getting gold and raking up riches which their avarice stimulated them so boundlessly to prosecute. They do not understand any more of a God, whether he be made of wood, brass or clay, than they did above a hundred years ago, New

Spain only exempted, which is a small part of America, and was visited and instructed by the religious. Thus they did formerly and still do perish without true faith or the knowledge and benefit of our religious sacraments.

"I Friar Bartholomeas De las Casas (or Casaus) of the Order of St. Dominick, who through the mercy of God arrived at the Spanish Court, cordially wish the expulsion of Hell or these hellish acts out of the Indies. Fearing least those souls redeemed by the precious blood of Christ, should perish eternally, but heartily desire that they may acknowledge their Creator and be saved; as also for the care and compassion that I ever had for my native country Castile, dreading least God should destroy it for the many sins committed by the natives her children, against faith, honor and their neighbors. I have at length upon the request of some many people in this court, who are fervently zealous of the honor of God and moved with pity at the calamities and afflictions of their neighbors (though I long since proposed it within my self and resolved to accomplish it, but could not, being distracted with the avocations of multiplicity of constant business and employment, have leisure to effect it) I say I have at length finished this treatise and summary at Valencia, Dec. 8th 1542, when they arrived at the height and utmost degree of executing violences, oppressions, tyranny, desolations, torments and calamities in all the said regions inhabited by the Spaniards (though they are more cruel in some places than others) yet Mexico with its confines were more favorably treated than the rest of the provinces.

And indeed no man dares to openly and publicly injure the inhabitants, for there is some justice (which is no where else in India) though very little is done and practiced; yet they are grievously taxed. I do really believe and am fully persuaded, that our sovereign Lord Charles the 5th, Emperor and King of Spain, our Lord and Prince, who begins to understand the wickedness and treacheries, which have been and still are committed against this miserable nation and distressed Countries, contrary to the will and pleasure of God, as well as His Majesties, that he will in time (for the truth has been concealed and kept from his knowledge with as great craft as fraud and malice) totally extirpate and root up all these evils and mischiefs, and apply proper medicines as may purge the morbid and piquant humors in the politics of this New World committed to his care and Government as a lover and promoter of peace and tranquility. God preserve and bless him with renown and happy life in his Imperial State, and prosper him in all his attempts, that he may fix the distempers of the Christian Church and crown him at last with eternal felicity, Amen."

After I published this treatise, certain laws and constitutions enacted by his Majesty then, at Barcelona in the month of December, An. Dom. 1542, promulgated and published the year ensuing in the City of Madera, whereby it is provided (as the present necessities required) that a period be put to such great enormities and sins, as were committed against God and our neighbors and tended to the utter ruin and perdition of this New World. These laws were published by his Majesties Order, several persons of highest authority, counselors, learned and conscientious men, being assembled together for that purpose, and many debates made at Valedolid about this weighty affair, with a unanimous consent and advice of all those who had given their opinions to writing, they were made public and traced more closely in the laws of Christ and Christianity, and were judged pure and free Persons of innocence of that stain and blemish of depriving the Indians of their treasures by theft and rape, which riches had contaminated and sullied the hands, but much more the souls of those who were enslaved by those heaps of wealth and covetousness, now this obstinate and hot pursuit after wealth was the original of all those evils committed without the least remorse or check of conscience.

These Laws being thus promulgated, the courtiers who promoted these Tyrants, took care that several copies should be transcribed (though they were extremely afflicted to see, that there was no farther hopes or means to promote the former depredations and extortions by the tyranny said) and sent them to several Indian Provinces. They, who took upon them the trouble and care of extirpating and oppressing by different ways of cruelty, as they never observed any method or order, but behaved themselves most inordinately and irregularly, having perused these diplomata or constitutions before the new made judges appointed to execute them could arrive, they by the assistance of those (as is credibly rumored, nor is it repugnant to truth) who favored their criminal and violent actions, knowing well that these Laws and Proclamations must necessarily take effect, began to grow mutinous and rebel, and when the Judges arrived, who were to execute these mandates, laying aside all manner of love and fear of god, were so audacious as to contemn and set not at all the reverence and obedience due to their King, and so became traitors, demeaning themselves like blood-thirsty tyrants, destitute and void of all humanity.

More particularly this appeared in the Peruvian Kingdoms, where An. Dom. 1542, they acted such horrid and stupendous enormities, that the like were never known or heard in America, or throughout the whole world before that time: Nor were they only practiced upon the Indians, who were mostly destroyed, but upon themselves also. God permitting them by his just Judgment to be their own executioners and sheath their swords in one another's bowels. In like manner, the other parts of this New World, being moved by the example of these rebels, refused to yield obedience to those Laws. The rest pretending to petition his Majesty turn rebellious themselves; for they would not voluntarily resign those estates, goods and chattels they have already usurped, nor willingly manumit those Indians, who were doomed to be their slaves, during life, and where they restrained the murdering sword from executing, they oppress them gradually with personal vassalage, unjust and intolerable burthens, which his Majesty could not possibly avert or hinder to, because they are all universally, some publicly and openly, others secretly, so naturally addicted to rob, thieve and steal. Thus under pretext of serving the King, they dishonor God and defraud his Imperial Majesty.

Here the Author having finished the matter of fact in this compendious history, for confirmation of what he has here written, quotes a tedious and imperfect epistle (as he styles it) beginning and ending anonymous with all containing the cruelties committed by the Spaniards, the same in effect as our Author has mentioned. Now in regard that I judge such reiterated cruelties and repeated barbarisms are offensive to the reader, he having sailed already too long and too far in an ocean of innocent Indian blood, I have omitted all but two or three stories not taken notice of by the Author. One of the Tyrants (who followed the steps of John Ampudia, a notorious villain) gave way to slaughter of sheep the chief food and support of the Spaniards as well as Indians, permitting them to kill two or three hundred at a time, only for their brains, fat or suet, whose flesh was then altogether useless and not fit to be eaten. But many Indians, the Spaniards friends and confederates followed them, desiring they might have the hearts to feed upon, where they butchered a great many of them, for this only reason, because they would not eat the other parts of the body. Two of their gang in the Province of Peru killed twenty five sheep, who were sold among the Spaniards for twenty five Crowns, merely to get the fat and brains out of them: Thus the frequent and extraordinary slaughter of their sheep, over a hundred thousand head of cattle were destroyed. And upon this account the Region was reduced to great penury and want and perished with hunger. The Province of Quito, which abounded with corn beyond expression, by such proceedings as these, was brought to that extremity that a small measure of wheat was sold for ten Crowns and a sheep at as dear a rate.

This Captain, taking leave of Quito, was followed by a poor Indianeass with loud cries and clamors, begging and beseeching him not to carry away her husband; for she had three children and could not possibly supply them with victuals, but they must inevitably die with hunger, and though the Captain repulsed her with an angry brow at the first; she approached him a second time with repeated cries, saying that her children must perish for want of food; but finding the Captain inexorable and altogether unmoved with her complaints and her husband not restored, through a piquant necessity wedded to despair; she cut off the heads of her children with sharp stones and so dispatched them into the other World.

Then he proceeded farther to another City and sent some Spaniards that very night, to take the Indians of the City of Tulilicui, who next day brought with them over a hundred Persons; some of which (whom he saw to be able to carry burthens) he reserved for his own and his soldiers service, and other were chained and perished in their fetters: but the little infants he gave to the Casic of Tulilicui, said to be eaten up and devoured, whose skins are stuffed with ashes and hung up in his house to be seen at this very day. And in the close of this letter he shuts up all with these words, is remarkable and never to be forgotten, that this Tyrant (being not ignorant of the mischiefs and enormities executed by him) boasting said of himself: "They who shall travel in these countries in fifty years and hear the things related of me, will have cause to say or declare, that never such a Tyrant as I am marched through these Regions and committed the like enormities"

Now not to quit the stage without one comical scene or action where such cruelties have been lively impersonated, give me leave to acquaint you with a comical piece of grammatical learning in a Reverend Religiosity of these parts, sent there to convert the West-Indies Pagans, which the Author mentions among his reasons and replications and all these I pass by as immaterial to our purpose, many of them being repeated in the narrative before.

The weight and burthen of initiating the Indians into the Christian faith lay solely on the Spaniards at first; and therefore Joannes Colmenero in Santa Martha, a fantastic, ignorant and foppish fellow, was under examination before us (and he had one of the most spacious cities committed to his charge as well as the care and cure of the souls of the inhabitants) whether he understood how to fortify himself with the sign of the Cross against the wicked and impious and being interrogated what he taught and how he instructed the Indians, whose souls were entrusted to his care and conduct; he returned this answer; That if he damned them to the devil and furies of Hell, it was sufficient to retrieve them, if he pronounced these words, *Per Signin Sanctin Cruces*. A fellow fitter to be a hog head than a shepherd of souls.

This deep, bloody American tragedy is now concluded and my pen chokes with Indian blood and gore. I have no more to say, but pronounce the Epilogue made by the author and leave the reader to judge whether it deserves a plaudit.

The Spaniards first set sail to America, not for the honor of God or as Persons moved and merited by servant zeal to the true faith, nor to promote the salvation of their neighbors, nor to serve the King, as they falsely boast and pretend to do, but in truth only stimulated and goaded on by insatiable greed and ambition, that they might for ever domineer, command and tyrannize over the West- Indians, whose Kingdoms they hoped to divide and distribute among themselves. Which to deal candidly, is no more or less intentionally than by all these indirect ways to disappoint and expel the Kings of Castile out of those dominions and territories, that they themselves having usurped the supreme and regal empire, might first challenge it as their right and then possess and enjoy it.

Recommended Readings

- The Teachings of Ptahhotep: The Oldest Book in the World

- The Five Negro Presidents: According to what White People Said They Were

- 100 Amazing Facts About the Negro with Complete Proof: A Short Cut to The World History of The Negro

- From Babylon to Timbuktu: A History of the Ancient Black Races Including the Black Hebrews

Available at www.bnpublishing.com